THE LAW OF CAPITAL PUNISHMENT

Second Edition

by

Margaret C. Jasper

Oceana's Legal Almanac Series:
Law for the Layperson

Oceana®
NEW YORK

OXFORD
UNIVERSITY PRESS

Oxford University Press, Inc., publishes works that further Oxford University's objective of excellence in research, scholarship, and education.

Copyright © 2008 by Oxford University Press, Inc.
Published by Oxford University Press, Inc.
198 Madison Avenue, New York, New York 10016

Library of Congress Cataloging-in-Publication Data

Jasper, Margaret C.
  The law of capital punishment / by Margaret C. Jasper.—2nd ed.
    p. cm.—(Oceana's legal almanac series. Law for the layperson,
ISSN 1075-7376)
  Includes bibliographical references.
  ISBN 978-0-19-537655-5 (alk. paper)
  1. Capital punishment—United States. I. Title. II. Series.
KF9227.C2J37 2008
345.73'0773—dc22

                                                              2008023829

Note to Readers:

This publication is designed to provide accurate and authoritative information in regard to the subject matter covered. It is based upon sources believed to be accurate and reliable and is intended to be current as of the time it was written. It is sold with the understanding that the publisher is not engaged in rendering legal, accounting, or other professional services. If legal advice or other expert assistance is required, the services of a competent professional person should be sought. Also, to confirm that the information has not been affected or changed by recent developments, traditional legal research techniques should be used, including checking primary sources where appropriate.

(Based on the Declaration of Principles jointly adopted by a Committee of the American Bar Association and a Committee of Publishers and Associations.)

You may order this or any other Oxford University Press publication by visiting the Oxford University Press website at www.oup.com

To My Husband Chris

Your love and support

are my motivation and inspiration

To My Sons, Michael, Nick and Chris

-and-

In memory of my son, Jimmy

Table of Contents

ABOUT THE AUTHOR ix
INTRODUCTION xiii

CHAPTER 1:
HISTORY AND OVERVIEW OF CAPITAL PUNISHMENT

IN GENERAL 1
RELIGIOUS VIEW OF CAPITAL PUNISHMENT. 2
HISTORY OF CAPITAL PUNISHMENT IN AMERICA. 3
  Ban on the Death Penalty in the United States 3
  Reintroduction of the Death Penalty in the United States. 3
  Chronology of the Death Penalty in America 4
PRESENT APPLICATION OF THE DEATH PENALTY 6
  Death Penalty Jurisdictions 6
  Statistics 6
CAPITAL OFFENSES. 7
THE ABOLITIONIST MOVEMENT. 7
PUBLIC OPINION 8
  In General 8
  Financial Concerns: Weighing the Costs. 8
    Life Imprisonment: A Less Costly Alternative. 9
  Deterrence. 11
    Suicide-by-Execution Syndrome 12
THE INTERNATIONAL STATUS OF CAPITAL PUNISHMENT 12
  In General 12
  The Trend Towards Abolishing the Death Penalty 12
  Countries That Have Abolished the Death Penalty for All Crimes. 13
  "Exceptional Crimes" Death Penalty Countries 13
  "De Facto" Abolitionist Countries 13
  Countries That Practice the Death Penalty (Retentionist Countries) . . . 13
  International Death Sentences and Executions 14

International Agreements to Abolish the Death Penalty 14
  The Sixth Protocol to the European Convention on Human Rights . . . 14
  The Second Optional Protocol to the American Convention on
  Human Rights to Abolish the Death Penalty 14
  The Protocol to the American Convention on Human Rights to
  Abolish the Death Penalty 15
Juvenile Offenders and the Death Penalty 15
  The United Nations Convention on the Rights of the Child 15

CHAPTER 2:
METHODS OF EXECUTION

EARLY METHODS OF EXECUTION 17
  Ling Chi: Death by a Thousand Cuts. 17
  Hanging, Drawing, and Quartering 17
  Breaking on the Wheel. 18
PRESENT-DAY METHODS OF EXECUTION 18
  In General 18
  Hanging. 18
  Firing Squad 19
  Electrocution. 20
  Lethal Gas 21
  Lethal Injection 21
    Baze v. Rees 22
THE ROLE OF THE EXECUTIONER. 23
VIEWING THE EXECUTION 23
  In General 23
  Victim Witnesses 24

CHAPTER 3:
THE FEDERAL DEATH PENALTY

IN GENERAL 25
METHODS OF EXECUTION 26
THE ANTI-DRUG ABUSE ACT OF 1988 (THE "DRUG KINGPIN"
STATUTE) 26
THE FEDERAL DEATH PENALTY ACT OF 1994 (THE "CRIME BILL
EXPANSION") 27
RACE AND THE FEDERAL DEATH PENALTY 28
PROCEDURE. 29
  Authorization 29
  Right to Legal Representation 29
  Appeal. 29
  Clemency. 29

COSTS. 30
    Prosecution 30
    Defense 30
NATIVE AMERICANS 30
U.S. MILITARY 30
    History. 30
    Demographics 31
    Prosecution 31
    The U.S. Disciplinary Barracks. 32
    Execution Procedure 33
    Authorized Witnesses 34

CHAPTER 4:
LEGAL REPRESENTATION

IN GENERAL 37
STATISTICS. 37
    State Prisoners 37
    Federal Prisoners 38
    Local Prisoners 38
QUALIFICATIONS AND COMPETENCY 38
U.S. SUPREME COURT CASES 39
    Strickland v. Washington 39
        Deficient Performance of Counsel 40
        Deficient Performance Prejudiced Defendant's Right to Fair Trial. . . . 40
    Williams v. Taylor 40
    Cockrell v. Burdine 41
    Bell v. Cone. 41
    Wiggins v. Smith. 41
    Florida v. Nixon 42
    Rompilla v. Beard 42
THE ADOPTION OF STANDARDS 43
    Alabama. 43
    Nevada. 43
    Texas 43
    Utah. 43
INDIGENT DEFENSE PROGRAMS. 43
    Public Defender Programs. 44
    Assigned Counsel Programs. 44
        The Ad Hoc Assigned Counsel Program. 44
        The Coordinated Assigned Counsel Program. 44
    Contract Attorney Programs. 44
    The Federal Indigent Defense Program 45

CHAPTER 5:
INNOCENCE

IN GENERAL 47
WRONGFUL CONVICTION AND EXECUTION. 48
  Contributing Factors 48
    Expansion of Capital Crimes 48
    Juror Bias 48
    Laboratory Mistakes 48
    Lack of Defense Funding. 48
    Narrowing of Appellate Rights in Capital Cases. 49
    Politics 49
    Unreliable Evidence 49
      Mistaken Eyewitness Testimony 49
      Unreliable Witnesses 50
      Unreliable Confessions. 50
DNA ACCESS LAWS 50
  The Justice For All Act of 2004 51
  Post-Conviction DNA Exonerations 51
  Recent Death Row Exoneration Cases 52
    Levon Jones. 52
    Glen Edward Chapman 52
    Kennedy Brewer 53
    Curtis McCarty. 53
    Ryan Matthews 53
    Nicholas Yarris 53
    Ray Krone. 54
    Charles Irvin Fain 54
    Frank Lee Smith 54
    Earl Washington 54
  Execution of Innocent Defendants 55
    Ruben Cantu 55
    Carlos DeLuna. 55
    Gary Graham. 55
    Larry Griffin 55
    Leonel Herrera 55
    Jesse Jacobs 56
    Leo Jones 56
    Robert Nelson. 56
    Joseph O'Dell 56
    David Spence. 56
    Cameron Willingham. 56
COMPENSATION FOR WRONGFUL INCARCERATION 57
MODEL PENAL CODE RECOMMENDATIONS 57

CHAPTER 6:
DEMOGRAPHICS

RACE AND THE DEATH PENALTY. 59
  Statistics 60
  The Race of the Victim. 60
WOMEN AND THE DEATH PENALTY. 61
  Statistics 61
  Executions. 61
AGE AND THE DEATH PENALTY. 62
  Juvenile Offenders. 62
    Thompson v. Oklahoma. 63
    Stanford v. Kentucky. 63
    Roper v. Simmons 64
EXECUTION OF THE ELDERLY. 64
  Statistics 65
  Causes. 65
  Clarence Ray Allen. 65
  John B. Nixon, Sr.. 66

CHAPTER 7:
MENTAL DISABILITIES AND THE DEATH PENALTY

IN GENERAL 67
MENTAL RETARDATION 67
  Mental Retardation Defined. 67
  The Ban on Execution of the Mentally Retarded. 67
  Atkins v. Virginia. 67
    Retribution. 68
    Deterrence 68
    Wrongful Execution 69
  The IQ Factor. 69
MENTAL ILLNESS 69
  Mental Illness Defined. 69
  Mental Disorders. 70
    Bipolar Disorder. 70
    Borderline Personality Disorder. 70
    Brain Damage 71
    Depression 71
    Dissociative Disorder 72
    Post-Traumatic Stress Disorder. 72
    Schizophrenia. 72
  Extending the Atkins Ruling to the Mentally Ill 72
  Recent Executions Involving the Mentally Ill .74
    Troy Kunkle (Schizophrenia) 74

Donald Beardslee (Severe Brain Damage). 75
Charles Singleton (Schizophrenia) 75
Kevin Zimmerman (Brain Injury) 75
Hung Thanh Le (PTSD) 76
Kelsey Patterson (Paranoid Schizophrenia) 76
Robert Bryan (Paranoid Schizophrenia/Brain Disease). 77
Stephen Vrabel (Paranoid Schizophrenia) 77
Kevin Hocker (Bipolar Disorder) 77
Mark Bailey (Bipolar Disorder) 78
FALSE CONFESSIONS AND THE MENTALLY IMPAIRED 78

CHAPTER 8:
SENTENCE REVIEW

IN GENERAL 79
AUTOMATIC REVIEW 79
FEDERAL HABEAS CORPUS REVIEW OF STATE CRIMINAL CONVICTIONS. . 80
In General 80
Jurisdiction 81
Case Processing Time 81
Representation 82
Types of Issues Raised in Habeas Corpus Petitions 82
Dismissal of the Petition 82
CLEMENCY 83
Authority to Grant Clemency 83
Recent Cases 84
John Spirko. 84
Jeffrey Leonard 84
Michael Boyd. 84
Kenneth Foster 84
Robin Lovitt 84
Arthur P. Baird II. 85
Michael Daniels 85
Broad Clemencies 85

APPENDICES

1: THE FLORIDA DEATH PENALTY STATUTE 87
2: TABLE OF NUMBER OF PRISONERS EXECUTED IN 2007, BY
   STATE. 91
3: TABLE OF NUMBER OF PRISONERS UNDER SENTENCE OF
   DEATH (FEDERAL/STATE) AS OF DECEMBER 31, 2006 95
4: TABLE OF NUMBER OF PRISONERS UNDER SENTENCE OF
   DEATH, BY YEAR (1953–2006). 99

5: TABLE OF NUMBER OF EXECUTIONS (1930–2007)............103
6: TABLE OF CAPITAL OFFENSES, BY STATE.....................107
7: TABLE OF FEDERAL CAPITAL OFFENSES, BY STATUTE...........111
8: DIRECTORY OF DEATH PENALTY ABOLITIONIST
   ORGANIZATIONS...115
9: TABLE OF COMPARISON OF MURDER RATES IN DEATH
   PENALTY STATES WITH MURDER RATES IN NON-DEATH
   PENALTY STATES (1990–2006)............................117
10: TABLE OF EXECUTION METHODS, BY STATE...................119
11: TABLE OF TOTAL NUMBER OF EXECUTIONS, BY STATE,
    AND METHODS OF EXECUTION (1976–2007) 123
12: TABLE OF STATES THAT HAVE ADOPTED QUALIFICATION
    STANDARDS FOR ATTORNEYS HANDLING CAPITAL CASES
    ON BEHALF OF INDIGENT DEFENDANTS......................127
13: TABLE OF DEATH ROW PRISONERS EXONERATED, BY STATE 135
14: TABLE OF DEATH ROW PRISONERS EXONERATED, BY YEAR.......137
15: TABLE OF NUMBER OF PRISONERS UNDER SENTENCE
    OF DEATH, BY RACE (1968–2006) 139
16: TABLE OF NUMBER OF WOMEN PRISONERS UNDER
    SENTENCE OF DEATH, BY RACE (FEDERAL/STATE)
    (AS OF DECEMBER 31, 2006).............................141
17: TABLE OF NUMBER OF PRISONERS UNDER SENTENCE OF
    DEATH, BY AGE (AS OF DECEMBER 31, 2006) 143
18: STATUTES DEFINING MENTAL RETARDATION FOR THE
    PURPOSE OF IMPOSITION OF THE DEATH PENALTY............145
19: DEFENDANTS WITH MENTAL RETARDATION EXECUTED
    SINCE THE REINSTATEMENT OF THE DEATH PENALTY..........155
20: DIRECTORY OF STATE GOVERNORS' OFFICES.................159

GLOSSARY 163
BIBLIOGRAPHY AND ADDITIONAL RESOURCES 173

ABOUT THE AUTHOR

MARGARET C. JASPER is an attorney engaged in the general practice of law in South Salem, New York, concentrating in the areas of personal injury and entertainment law. Ms. Jasper holds a Juris Doctor degree from Pace University School of Law, White Plains, New York, is a member of the New York and Connecticut bars, and is certified to practice before the United States District Courts for the Southern and Eastern Districts of New York, the United States Court of Appeals for the Second Circuit, and the United States Supreme Court.

Ms. Jasper has been appointed to the law guardian panel for the Family Court of the State of New York, is a member of a number of professional organizations and associations, and is a New York State licensed real estate broker operating as Jasper Real Estate, in South Salem, New York.

Margaret Jasper maintains a website at http://www.JasperLawOffice.com.

In 2004, Ms. Jasper successfully argued a case before the New York Court of Appeals, which gives mothers of babies who are stillborn due to medical negligence the right to bring a legal action and recover emotional distress damages. This successful appeal overturned a 26-year old New York case precedent, which previously prevented mothers of stillborn babies from suing their negligent medical providers.

Ms. Jasper is the author and general editor of the following legal Almanacs:

AIDS Law

The Americans with Disabilities Act

Animal Rights Law

Auto Leasing

Bankruptcy Law for the Individual Debtor

Banks and their Customers

Becoming a Citizen

Buying and Selling Your Home

Commercial Law

Consumer Rights and the Law

Co-ops and Condominiums: Your Rights and Obligations as Owner

Copyright Law

Credit Cards and the Law

Custodial Rights

Dealing with Debt

Dictionary of Selected Legal Terms

Drunk Driving Law

DWI, DUI and the Law

Education Law

Elder Law

Employee Rights in the Workplace

Employment Discrimination Under Title VII

Environmental Law

Estate Planning

Everyday Legal Forms

Executors and Personal Representatives: Rights and Responsibilities

Guardianship and the Law

Harassment in the Workplace

Health Care and Your Rights

Health Care Directives

Hiring Household Help and Contractors: Your Rights and Obligations Under the Law

Home Mortgage Law Primer

Hospital Liability Law

How to Change Your Name

How to Form an LLC

How to Protect Your Challenged Child

How to Start Your Own Business

Identity Theft and How to Protect Yourself

Individual Bankruptcy and Restructuring

Injured on the Job: Employee Rights, Worker's Compensation and Disability Insurance Law

International Adoption

Juvenile Justice and Children's Law

Labor Law

Landlord-Tenant Law

Law for the Small Business Owner

The Law of Adoption

The Law of Attachment and Garnishment

The Law of Buying and Selling

The Law of Capital Punishment

The Law of Child Custody

The Law of Contracts

The Law of Debt Collection

The Law of Dispute Resolution

The Law of Immigration

The Law of Libel and Slander

The Law of Medical Malpractice

The Law of No-Fault Insurance

The Law of Obscenity and Pornography

The Law of Personal Injury

The Law of Premises Liability

The Law of Product Liability

The Law of Speech and the First Amendment

Lemon Laws

Living Together: Practical Legal Issues

Marriage and Divorce

Missing and Exploited Children: How to Protect Your Child

Motor Vehicle Law

Nursing Home Negligence

Patent Law

Pet Law

Planes, Trains and Buses: Your Rights as a Passenger

Prescription Drugs

Privacy and the Internet: Your Rights and Expectations Under the Law

Probate Law

Protecting Your Business: Disaster Preparation and the Law

Real Estate Law for the Homeowner and Broker

Religion and the Law

Retirement Planning

The Right to Die

Rights of Single Parents

Small Claims Court

Social Security Law

Special Education Law

Teenagers and Substance Abuse

Trademark Law

Trouble Next Door: What to do With Your Neighbor

Veterans' Rights and Benefits

Victim's Rights Law

Violence Against Women

Welfare: Your Rights and the Law

What if It Happened to You: Violent Crimes and Victims' Rights

What if the Product Doesn't Work: Warranties & Guarantees

Workers' Compensation Law

Your Child's Legal Rights: An Overview

Your Rights in a Class Action Suit

Your Rights as a Tenant

Your Rights Under the Family and Medical Leave Act

You've Been Fired: Your Rights and Remedies

INTRODUCTION

Over the past thirty years, the reintroduction of capital punishment in the United States has steadily increased. Presently, the death penalty is authorized by 36 states, the federal government, and the U.S. military. In addition, the federal government has recently expanded its application of the death penalty to a number of federal offenses.

Nevertheless, the general worldwide trend has been towards abolition of the death penalty, and more than 100 countries have done away with capital punishment either by law or by practice.

This Almanac sets forth an overview of capital punishment in the United States, including the reasons, which led to its abolition by the U.S. Supreme Court in 1972, and its subsequent reappearance in 1976. This Almanac examines the statistical application of the death penalty according to characteristics such as age, gender, and race, and the methods by which executions are carried out among the states.

The arguments for and against capital punishment are presented, including legal representation, deterrence, cost and the concern over unjustified executions of innocent individuals. Finally, this Almanac discusses the international status of the death penalty among abolitionist and retentionist countries.

The Appendix provides applicable statutes, resource directories, sample forms, and other pertinent information and data. The Glossary contains definitions of many of the terms used throughout the Almanac.

CHAPTER 1:
HISTORY AND OVERVIEW OF CAPITAL PUNISHMENT

IN GENERAL

Capital punishment—also referred to as the "death penalty"—is defined as the execution of a person by the state as punishment for certain specified crimes, known as capital offenses. The term is derived from the Latin word *capitalis*, which means "regarding the head," and originally referred to the execution of a person by decapitation.

According to historical records, the death penalty was used as punishment since the beginning of recorded history, and was a common part of the earliest known justice systems, however primitive they may have been.

Historically, capital punishment was used by almost all societies to both punish crime and suppress political dissent. For example, execution was widely employed as a means of oppressing political dissent by fascist or communist governments. Throughout history, the death penalty was the punishment for a wide range of crimes. In eighteenth century Britain, you could be executed for any one of 222 crimes, including stealing an animal or cutting down a tree.

In most places where the death penalty is still legal, including the United States, capital punishment is only used as punishment for crimes involving murder under certain circumstances, treason, and espionage.

Nevertheless, there are still some countries where a number of other offenses may result in the death penalty, including adultery, sodomy, rape, drug trafficking, human trafficking, and corruption. Certain military tribunals also allow for the execution of prisoners convicted of cowardice, insubordination, mutiny, and desertion, in order to maintain military discipline.

RELIGIOUS VIEW OF CAPITAL PUNISHMENT

Many religions have historically authorized the death penalty under certain circumstances. For example, according to the Old Testament, execution was the punishment for blasphemy, adultery, kidnapping, and violating the Sabbath, among other offenses. In practice, however, Judaism has abolished capital punishment through various Talmudic decisions.

In Christianity, there has been much controversy over whether the death penalty is permitted. The use of certain New Testament scriptures have been used to support its application, as well as to support its abolition. Worldwide, there is a movement against the death penalty within the Christian community.

Most Protestant Churches, including the Anglicans, Episcopalians, Methodists, Evangelical Lutherans, Mennonites, and Quakers, have condemned the death penalty. The Mormons have taken a neutral position on capital punishment; however, some Protestant churches still maintain that there is a scriptural basis in support of the death penalty.

The Roman Catholic Church historically accepted execution as a method of deterrence and prevention; however, the modern day position is that the death penalty is only permitted out of necessity, e.g., to defend human life against an unjust aggressor. Nevertheless, the Church has recognized that crime prevention and punishment has become the responsibility of the state.

There is controversy among Buddhist nations as to whether capital punishment is forbidden. Some interpret the Buddhist scriptures as contained in the Dhammapada—the Path of the Dharma—as denouncing the death penalty. Nevertheless, capital punishment is the law in those countries where Buddhism is the official or majority religion, including Thailand, Mongolia, and Sri Lanka.

Islam explicitly endorses the death penalty, although the victim or the victim's family may pardon the offender. The Koran condones capital punishment for certain crimes, including rape, treason, adultery, and homosexuality. Nevertheless, murder—the one crime that qualifies as a capital offense in all death penalty jurisdictions—is not one of the crimes listed in the Koran. Instead, murder is a civil crime subject to retaliation by the victim's family, who decides whether the offender's punishment will be execution or, alternatively, some sort of compensation to the family.

HISTORY OF CAPITAL PUNISHMENT IN AMERICA

The death penalty has been utilized as a form of punishment in America since colonial times. According to the Espy File, a database of executions in the United States and the earlier colonies from 1608 through 2002, there were 15,269 executions. The historical leaders in executions during that time period were Virginia (1375), Texas (1152), New York (1130), Pennsylvania (1043), and Georgia (990).

The greatest number of executions in the United States took place during the nineteenth and early twentieth centuries, when the public execution of criminals was common. One of the last public executions was conducted in 1936, when 20,000 people gathered to watch the hanging of a young black male in Kentucky. By the early 1960s, most states had stopped enforcing the death penalty.

Ban on the Death Penalty in the United States

In 1972, the United States Supreme Court held that the death penalty was cruel and unusual punishment in violation of the Eighth and Fourteenth Amendments to the U.S. Constitution (*Georgia v. Furman*, 408 U.S. 238 (1972)). Prior to *Furman*, the constitutionality of the death penalty was rarely challenged.

This landmark holding was based on a review of the existing capital punishment statutes. The Supreme Court did not find the practice itself to be unconstitutional, but rather the arbitrary and unpredictable manner in which the sentences were being imposed.

The Court concluded that the evidence proved the death penalty was being sought and/or handed down primarily in cases where the offender was poor, or a member of a minority group, and that death sentences were being imposed without any statutory guidelines or standards. As part of its decision, the Court reversed death sentences in many pending cases involving a variety of state statutes.

Reintroduction of the Death Penalty in the United States

In response to the *Furman* decision, a number of states rewrote their death penalty statutes in order to satisfy the scrutiny of the Court. In 1976, the Supreme Court lifted its ban on capital punishment, holding that its previous concerns with the unfair and arbitrary application of the death sentence had been addressed by the redrafted state statutes (*Gregg v. Georgia*, 428 U.S. 153 (1976)).

Since the reinstatement of the death penalty in 1976, there have been 1,099 executions in the United States as of October 2007, 53 of which were performed in 2006.

Florida, Georgia, and Texas were among the first state statutes to survive the Supreme Court's scrutiny. The Court held that these statutes provided the necessary guidance to prevent the arbitrary application of the death penalty by trial juries.

The text of the Florida Death Penalty Statute may be found in Appendix 1 of this Almanac.

Although the specific death penalty provisions of state statutes vary greatly, the typical statute now requires a bifurcated trial in capital cases—i.e., one which is divided into two components. During the first stage, the jury determines guilt or innocence.

If the defendant is judged innocent, the trial is over. If the defendant is found guilty, the trial proceeds to its second stage, at which point the jury—or in some states, the judge—chooses imprisonment or death in light of any aggravating or mitigating circumstances.

Chronology of the Death Penalty in America

According to the Congressional Quarterly Researcher, following is the chronology of the death penalty in America:

17th Century—England prescribes death for 14 offenses, but the American colonies impose the death sentence for fewer crimes.

1636—The Massachusetts Bay Colony lists 13 crimes punishable by death, including idolatry and witchcraft.

1682—Under William Penn's Great Act, the death penalty is prescribed only for murder and treason in Pennsylvania.

19th Century—Politics and advances in technology influence use of the death penalty.

Dec. 2, 1859—Abolitionist John Brown is hanged for treason, conspiracy and murder at Charles Town, Virginia.

Aug. 6, 1890—Murderer William Kemmler is the first person executed in the electric chair, at New York's Auburn Prison. The "chair" is later installed at Sing Sing Prison.

1900s—A short-lived abolition movement leads to the repeal of numerous state death penalty statutes.

1907—Kansas abolishes capital punishment. Eight more states follow suit over the next 10 years.

1920s—Two sensational murder cases spark renewed debate over the death penalty.

Sept 10, 1924—Defense attorney Clarence Darrow wins life sentences for Chicago "thrill killers" Richard Loeb and Nathan Leopold Jr.

Aug. 22, 1927—Nicola Sacco and Bartolomeo Vanzetti, Italian immigrants with anarchist sympathies, are electrocuted in Massachusetts for two murders.

1930s—U.S. executions reach an all-time peak, averaging 167 a year.

1960s—Growing doubts about the death penalty lead to a decline in executions.

June 2, 1967—After Luis Jose Monge dies in the gas chamber at Colorado State Penitentiary, an unofficial moratorium on executions begins.

1970s—An eventful decade for capital punishment sees the death penalty invalidated and then reinstated.

June 29, 1972—Supreme Court rules in *Furman v. Georgia* that the death penalty amounts to cruel and unusual punishment because juries impose sentences arbitrarily. The decision overturns all existing death penalty laws and death sentences

July 2, 1976—The Supreme Court holds in *Gregg v. Georgia* that under the state's new two-stage trial system, the death penalty no longer violates the Eighth Amendment.

January 17, 1977—A Utah firing squad makes Gary Gilmore the first person executed in the U.S. in almost 10 years.

1977—Oklahoma becomes the first state to adopt lethal injection.

1980s—The Supreme Court further clarifies its views on the death penalty.

1986—Supreme Court bars executing insane persons in *Ford v. Wainwright*.

1989—In *Perry v. Lynaugh*, the Supreme Court holds that executing mentally retarded persons does not violate the Eighth Amendment.

1990s—Death Penalty provisions in anti-crime bills stir sharp debate in Congress.

Sept. 13, 1994—President Clinton signs crime bill making dozens of federal crimes subject to the death penalty.

Feb. 8, 1995—The House votes 297-132 to limit inmate appeals of death sentences to one year in state cases.

March 7, 1995—New York Governor George E. Pataki signs new death penalty law.

PRESENT APPLICATION OF THE DEATH PENALTY

Death Penalty Jurisdictions

As of March 1, 2008, the death penalty was authorized by 36 states, the federal government, and the U.S. Military. The state and federal death penalty statutes are patterned after those the Supreme Court upheld in *Gregg v. Georgia.*

Those jurisdictions without the death penalty include 14 states and the District of Columbia, including: Alaska, Hawaii, Iowa, Maine, Massachusetts, Michigan, Minnesota, New Jersey, New York, North Dakota, Rhode Island, Vermont, West Virginia, and Wisconsin.

Statistics

As of October 1, 2007, since the death penalty was reinstated in 1976, 1,099 convicted murderers have been executed in the United States. Those executions took place in 33 different states. A total of 405 (37%) of those executions took place in Texas.

In 2007, 42 persons in 10 states were executed, including 26 in Texas; 3 each in Oklahoma and Alabama; 2 each in Alaska, Ohio, and Tennessee; and 1 each in South Dakota, Georgia, South Carolina, and Arizona. Of this total, 28 of the executed prisoners were white and 14 were black. All of the executed prisoners were men.

Lethal injection was used in 41 of the executions in 2007, and the remaining execution was carried out by electrocution.

In addition, 3,350 prisoners were under sentence of death as of February 2008.

A table setting forth the number of prisoners executed in 2007, categorized by state, may be found in Appendix 2 of this Almanac.

A table setting forth the number of prisoners under sentence of death at the end of 2006, categorized by state, may be found in Appendix 3 of this Almanac.

A table setting forth the number of prisoners under sentence of death from 1953 through 2006 may be found in Appendix 4 of this Almanac.

A table setting forth the number of executions conducted from 1930 through 2007 may be found in Appendix 5 of this Almanac.

CAPITAL OFFENSES

Crimes that may result in the death penalty are called capital offenses. In the United States, capital offenses are reserved as punishment for serious crimes, such as premeditated murder.

Almost all state capital punishment statutes differ with respect to which crimes constitute capital offenses. For example, some states—such as Delaware—limit the death penalty to first-degree murder, while other states—such as Mississippi—may hand down a death sentence for other crimes, such as aircraft piracy.

A table of capital offenses categorized by state is set forth at Appendix 6.

In addition, the federal government has statutorily authorized the death penalty for a number of additional offenses, including espionage and treason.

A table of federal capital offenses categorized by statute is set forth at Appendix 7.

THE ABOLITIONIST MOVEMENT

Although there has been a definite rise in death penalty sentencing in the United States since 1976, there has also been a strong counter-movement towards its abolition by certain organized groups such as Amnesty International (AI) and the American Civil Liberties Union (ACLU). In addition, Catholic, Jewish, and Protestant religious groups are among the more than 50 national organizations that constitute the National Coalition to Abolish the Death Penalty (NCADP).

All abolitionist groups generally adhere to the ACLU position that the death penalty inherently violates the constitutional ban against cruel and unusual punishment and the guarantees of due process and equal protection under the law. They believe that states should not have the right to ceremonially kill in the name of justice, and that capital punishment is inconsistent with the fundamental values of our democratic system.

In addition, it is argued that despite efforts to rewrite the statutes, the application of the death penalty is necessarily arbitrary under our criminal justice system. In support of their position, they offer statistical evidence demonstrating that the death penalty is imposed disproportionately upon offenders who are poor, uneducated, or minorities.

In further support of abolition, it is argued that once a death sentence is carried out, it is clearly irrevocable if exculpatory evidence is subsequently uncovered. In that connection, abolitionist organizations attempt to prevent executions and abolish the death penalty through litigation, legislation, and public awareness efforts.

A directory of organizations that support abolition of capital punishment is set forth at Appendix 8.

PUBLIC OPINION

In General

In May 2006, a Gallup Poll showed death penalty support in the United States at 65%, down from the 74% approval a year earlier. Despite overwhelming anti-death penalty media saturation, 51% believe that the death penalty is not imposed often enough; 60% believe that the death penalty is applied fairly, and when given a choice to name the better penalty for murder, "life imprisonment with absolutely no possibility of parole" is preferred over the death penalty 48% to 47%.

Thus, capital punishment continues to be a controversial issue in the United States as well as the rest of the world. Abolitionists oppose the death penalty for religious, moral, emotional, and practical reasons. Many citizens overwhelmingly support the death penalty for serious crimes such as intentional murder. As a result, the death penalty has become an important political issue in national, state, local, and even judicial elections.

The majority of states, acting on what they believe to be the will of the people, have statutorily provided for capital punishment. In addition, the federal government responded by expanding the federal death penalty and eliminating federal funding to death penalty resource centers, which were dedicated to defending death row prisoners, and instrumental in the release of a number of wrongly convicted prisoners on death row.

Many reasons have been given for supporting the death penalty, the least legitimate of which is the desire for revenge. The biblical adage—"An eye for an eye and a tooth for a tooth"—is often cited during discussions on capital punishment.

As discussed below, the two primary arguments supporting the death penalty are: (1) Financial Concerns; and (2) Deterrence.

Financial Concerns: Weighing the Costs

Death penalty advocates argue that executing a prisoner is far less expensive than paying for the offender's upkeep in prison for the rest of his or her life, and that abolishing capital punishment is thus unfair to the taxpayer. However, if one takes into account all the relevant costs associated with prosecuting a death penalty case to its conclusion, the opposite is true. In fact, many state studies have demonstrated that capital punishment is a very expensive program to administer, and far exceeds the cost of life imprisonment.

For example, a murder trial is usually much more protracted when the death penalty is an issue. Further, a significant delay between the imposition of a death sentence and the actual execution is inevitable given the procedural safeguards required in capital cases. Post-conviction appeals in death-penalty cases are far more frequent than in any other cases.

The costs of litigation can also be tremendous, taking into consideration the time spent by judges, prosecutors, court reporters, defense counsel, jurors, and other court personnel. And, the instrumentalities needed to carry out an execution add further expense. For example, the Federal Bureau of Prisons recently constructed one lethal injection chamber in Terre Haute, Indiana, at a cost of approximately $500,000.

Life Imprisonment: A Less Costly Alternative

As set forth below, a number of state and national studies have been conducted which support the argument that life imprisonment is a less costly alternative to capital punishment. However, a major criticism of sentencing the offender to a jail sentence is that "life imprisonment," does not always mean the offender spends life in prison, e.g., due to parole, shortened sentences, etc. In addition, the recidivism rate—i.e., the number of parolees and ex-convicts that re-offend—is disturbing and dangerous.

The most comprehensive cost study was undertaken in North Carolina by Duke University in 1993. The study concluded that pursuing a death penalty conviction costs North Carolina $2.16 million per execution more than the cost of a non-death penalty murder case with a sentence of life imprisonment.

There have been similar findings in other states where the death penalty has been vigorously sought:

1. California—According to a 2005 story published in The Los Angeles Times, state and federal records demonstrated that the California death penalty system costs taxpayers more than $114 million a year beyond the cost of life imprisonment.

2. Florida—According to a 2000 report published in The Palm Beach Post, Florida would save $51 million each year by punishing all first-degree murderers with life in prison without parole instead of pursuing the death penalty.

3. Indiana—According to a 2002 study by the Indiana Criminal Law Study Commission, the total cost of prosecuting a capital case is 38% greater than the total cost of life without parole sentences.

4. Kansas—The Kansas Death Penalty Cost Report conducted in 2003 concluded that capital cases are substantially more expensive than comparable non-death penalty cases. The median cost of a death penalty case was $1.26 million, whereas the median cost of a non-death penalty case was $740,000.

5. New Jersey—According to a 2005 report published by the New Jerseyans for Alternatives to the Death Penalty (NJADP), New Jersey spent $253.3 million on its death penalty system since the state reinstated capital punishment in 1982 until its abolition. This figure included prosecution costs ($180 million); defense costs ($60 million); court costs ($6.5 million); and Department of Corrections costs ($6.8 million).

6. Tennessee—According to a 2004 report released by the Tennessee Comptroller of the Treasury, death penalty trials cost an average of 48% more than the average cost of trials in which prosecutors seek life imprisonment.

7. Washington—According to a 2006 report to the Washington State Bar, at the trial level, death penalty cases are estimated to generate roughly $470,000 in additional costs to the prosecution and defense as compared to the cost of a murder trial without the death penalty. In addition, court personnel costs range from $47,000 to $70,000. On direct appeal, the cost of defense averages $100,000 more in death penalty cases, than in non-death penalty murder cases.

Nationally, according to a 2001 report released by the National Bureau of Economic Research, the extra cost of capital trials between 1982 and 1997 was $1.6 billion dollars. The study concluded that counties manage these high costs by decreasing funding for highways and police, and by increasing taxes. In addition, abolitionists argue that this money could have been better spent on programs designed to reduce crime.

Although supporters of the death penalty have also denounced the additional costs of prosecuting capital cases, the only way to make a death penalty case less expensive would be to limit the defendant's appellate rights. The result, however, would be to put many prisoners on death row who should not justifiably be executed.

As further set forth in Chapter 5, Innocence, a number of innocent individuals would have been executed had they not been able to exercise their constitutionally guaranteed right to due process in order to demonstrate their innocence.

In fact, almost half of the death penalty cases reviewed under federal habeas corpus provisions resulted in a reversal of the death sentence. Federal habeas corpus is discussed further in Chapter 8, Sentence Review, of this Almanac.

Deterrence

The primary motivation underlying capital punishment is the logical notion that the threat of execution will prevent or discourage criminal behavior. Proponents of the death penalty argue that it sends a strong message to other potential criminals. Advocates of the death penalty also point out that executing the offender necessarily prevents him or her from committing further crimes.

Although the death penalty necessarily guarantees that the condemned person will commit no further crimes, studies have shown that the death penalty has not had any appreciable deterrent effect on other criminals.

The explanations for this failed objective include the following:

1. A punishment can be an effective deterrent only if it is consistently and expeditiously undertaken. Capital punishment cannot be administered to meet these conditions unless a defendant is stripped of his or her constitutional rights.

2. The proportion of first-degree murderers under sentence of death is relatively small. An even smaller subset of this group have actually been executed. According to law enforcement authorities, death sentences imposed for murder only account for approximately 1% of all known homicides.

3. Most capital crimes are not premeditated—i.e., they are not planned. Thus, it is not plausible that the threat of punishment could deter a crime that usually occurs in the heat of the moment. In such cases, individuals often act without considering the consequences.

4. Terrorists often commit violent crime on behalf of strong religious, moral or political beliefs which tend to outweigh any concern for personal safety, and for which martyrdom is honorable.

5. Illegal drug traffickers are already involved in a dangerous and violent business in which the threat of death is a day-to-day reality whereas the remote threat of death as a criminal justice penalty is more illusive.

Studies have demonstrated that the death penalty is no more effective than incarceration in deterring murder, the primary offense for which most states impose a death sentence. In fact, according to the Federal Bureau of Investigation, from 1990 to 2006, states without the death penalty had a consistently lower homicide rate than death penalty states.

For example, in 2006, the murder rate per 100,000 in death penalty states was 5.9 compared to 4.22 in non-death penalty cases, a difference of 40%.

A table setting forth the murder rate in death penalty states compared to non-death penalty states (1990–2006) is set forth at Appendix 9.

Suicide-by-Execution Syndrome

Abolitionists argue that in some instances the death penalty actually incites the capital crime it is supposed to deter. In support of this notion, they point to clinically documented cases of the so-called "suicide-by-execution syndrome."

This syndrome involves individuals who would like to commit suicide but fear actually taking their own life. Thus, they commit murder for the sole purpose of having the death sentence imposed upon them.

THE INTERNATIONAL STATUS OF CAPITAL PUNISHMENT

In General

While the U.S. has been expanding the number of death penalty eligible crimes, limiting appellate rights, and moving towards swifter executions, the international community has been moving away from the death penalty. As indicated below, the death penalty has been abolished, either by law or practice, in most countries.

The Trend Towards Abolishing the Death Penalty

Since 1976, an average of two countries a year have abolished the death penalty, particularly for ordinary crimes. Capital punishment has been abolished, in law or in practice, in over one hundred countries worldwide.

The United Nations (UN) has called upon member states to abolish the death penalty, and the Vatican has condemned the widespread use of the death penalty. In addition, new countries joining the Council of Europe, including many former communist countries, have pledged to abolish the death penalty.

According to Amnesty International (AI), 91 countries and territories have abolished the death penalty for all crimes; 11 countries have abolished the death penalty for all but exceptional crimes, e.g., wartime crimes; and 33 countries are abolitionist "de facto"—i.e., they retain the death penalty in law but have not carried out any executions for the past 10 years or more; are believed to have a policy or established practice of not carrying out executions; and/or have made an international commitment not to use the death penalty.

Countries That Have Abolished the Death Penalty for All Crimes

Countries which have abolished the death penalty include: Albania, Andorra, Angola, Armenia, Australia, Austria, Azerbaijan, Belgium, Bhutan, Bosnia-Herzegovina, Cambodia, Canada, Cape Verde, Colombia, Costa Rica, Cote D'Ivoire, Croatia, Cyprus, Czech Republic, Denmark, Djibouti, Dominican Republic, Ecuador, Estonia, Finland, France, Georgia, Germany, Greece, Guinea-Bissau, Haiti, Honduras, Hungary, Iceland, Ireland, Italy, Kiribati, Liberia, Liechtenstein, Lithuania, Luxembourg, Macedonia, Malta, Marshall Islands, Mauritius, Mexico, Micronesia, Moldova, Monaco, Montenegro, Mozambique, Namibia, Nepal, Netherlands, New Zealand, Nicaragua, Niue, Norway, Palau, Paraguay, Philippines, Poland, Portugal, Romania, Rwanda, Samoa, San Marino, Sao Tome and Principe, Senegal, Serbia, Seychelles, Slovakia, Slovenia, Solomon Islands, South Africa, Spain, Sweden, Switzerland, Timor-Leste, Turkey, Turkmenistan, Tuvalu, Ukraine, United Kingdom, Uruguay, Uzbekistan, Vanuatu, Vatican City State, and Venezuela.

"Exceptional Crimes" Death Penalty Countries

The following countries have retained the death penalty, but apply it only for what are determined to be "exceptional crimes"—e.g., military crimes or crimes under emergency laws: Argentina, Bolivia, Brazil, Chile, Cook Islands, El Salvador, Fiji, Israel, Kyrgyzstan, Latvia, and Peru.

"De Facto" Abolitionist Countries

The following countries are considered "abolitionist de facto," in that they retain the death penalty in law—"de jure"—but have not executed anyone for the past 10 years, or have declared a moratorium on executions: Algeria, Benin, Brunei Darussalam, Burkina Faso, Central African Republic, Congo (Republic), Eritrea, Gabon, Gambia, Ghana, Grenada, Kenya, Laos, Madagascar, Malawi, Maldives, Mali, Mauritania, Morocco, Myanmar, Nauru, Niger, Papua New Guinea, Russian Federation, South Korea, Sri Lanka, Suriname, Swaziland, Tanzania, Togo, Tonga, Tunisia, and Zambia.

Countries That Practice the Death Penalty (Retentionist Countries)

The following countries retain the death penalty both in law and in practice: Afghanistan, Antigua and Barbuda, Bahamas, Bahrain, Bangladesh,

Barbados, Belarus, Belize, Botswana, Burundi, Cameroon, Chad, China, Comoros, Congo (Democratic Republic), Cuba, Dominica, Egypt, Equatorial Guinea, Ethiopia, Guatemala, Guinea, Guyana, India, Indonesia, Iran, Iraq, Jamaica, Japan, Jordan, Kazakhstan, Kuwait, Lebanon, Lesotho, Libya, Lithuania, Malaysia, Mongolia, Nigeria, North Korea, Oman, Pakistan, Palestinian Authority, Qatar, Saint Christopher & Nevis, St. Lucia, St. Vincent & Grenadines, Saudi Arabia, Sierra Leone, Singapore, Somalia, Sudan, , Syria, Taiwan, Tajikistan, Thailand, Trinidad and Tobago, Uganda, United Arab Emirates, United States of America, Vietnam, Yemen, and Zimbabwe.

International Death Sentences and Executions

In 2006, there were 1,591 executions around the world. Amnesty International reported that executions worldwide fell by more than 25% in 2006, down from 2,148 in 2005. Of all known executions that took place in 2006, 91% were carried out in six countries: China (1,010), Iran (177), Pakistan (82), Iraq (65), Sudan (65), and the United States (53).

International Agreements to Abolish the Death Penalty

One of the most important developments in recent years has been the adoption of international treaties whereby countries commit to abolishing their death penalty.

Three such treaties now exist, including: (1) The Sixth Protocol to the European Convention on Human Rights; (2) The Second Optional Protocol to the International Covenant on Civil and Political Rights; and (3) The Protocol to the American Convention on Human Rights to Abolish the Death Penalty.

The Sixth Protocol to the European Convention on Human Rights

The Sixth Protocol to the European Convention on Human Rights is an agreement to abolish the death penalty in peacetime to which 18 countries had signed on by mid-1995. The other two protocols provide for the total abolition of the death penalty but allow countries wishing to do so to retain the death penalty in wartime as an exception.

The Second Optional Protocol to the American Convention on Human Rights to Abolish the Death Penalty

In its Second Optional Protocol to the International Covenant on Civil and Political Rights, the United Nations has declared that abolition of the death penalty will enhance human dignity and assist in the development of human rights.

The Protocol to the American Convention on Human Rights to Abolish the Death Penalty

The Protocol to the American Convention on Human Rights to Abolish the Death Penalty was adopted at Asuncion, Paraguay on June 8, 1990. While Article 4 of the American Convention had already placed severe restrictions on the member states' ability to impose the death penalty, signing this protocol formalizes a state's solemn commitment to refrain from using capital punishment in any peacetime circumstance. To date, it has been ratified by Brazil, Costa Rica, Ecuador, Nicaragua, Panama, Paraguay, Uruguay, and Venezuela.

Juvenile Offenders and the Death Penalty

Internationally, the death penalty for juvenile offenders—i.e., those prisoners who were under age 18 at the time they committed the crime—is rare. Since 1990, eight countries, including China, the Democratic Republic of Congo, Iran, Nigeria, Pakistan, Saudi Arabia, Yemen, and the United States of America, have executed defendants who were juveniles at the time of their crime.

In addition, since 1990, each of those countries has either abolished the death penalty for juveniles or publicly disavowed the practice. However, the United States and Somalia have not yet ratified Article 37 of the United Nations Convention on the Rights of the Child, which expressly prohibits capital punishment for crimes committed by juveniles, as set forth below.

The United Nations Convention on the Rights of the Child

The United Nations Convention on the Rights of the Child (UNCRC) is an international convention that sets forth the civil, political, economic, social and cultural rights of children. It is composed of members from countries around the world, and is monitored by the United Nations Committee on the Rights of the Child. All member nations of the United Nations, except the United States and Somalia, have ratified the UNCRC.

The UNCRC generally defines a child as any person under the age of 18. Among its other provisions, Article 37(a) of the UNCRC forbids capital punishment for children. In addition, Article 37(a) also prohibits sentencing juveniles to life imprisonment with no opportunity for parole:

UNRC—Article 37(a)

States Parties shall ensure that:

(a) No child shall be subjected to torture or other cruel, inhuman or degrading treatment or punishment. Neither capital punishment nor life imprisonment without possibility of release shall be imposed for offences committed by persons below eighteen years of age.

CHAPTER 2:
METHODS OF EXECUTION

EARLY METHODS OF EXECUTION

According to historical records, the earliest executions were often carried out in cruel and inhuman ways. Many criminals were boiled, disemboweled, crucified, impaled, crushed, stoned, burned, dismembered, decapitated, and slowly sliced to death.

Ling Chi: Death by a Thousand Cuts

In China, from the year 900 until it was abolished in 1905, a method of execution called *Ling Chi* ("death by a thousand cuts") was a commonly used punishment for murder and treason. Reportedly, *Ling Chi* was carried out by first cutting out the prisoner's eyes, so as to increase his terror. The executioner would use the sharp blade to make increasingly larger cuts to the prisoner's body until he died. Depending on the order in which the body parts were cut, the execution could last for minutes or days. The body was then put on public display.

Hanging, Drawing, and Quartering

Perhaps one of the most heinous methods of capital punishment was practiced in Britain until the early 19th century. Hanging, drawing, and quartering was a punishment reserved for those who committed treason, a crime often viewed as worse than murder. This horrific practice involved hanging the prisoner until he was almost dead, placing the prisoner on the quartering table, removing his genitalia and intestines and burning them before their eyes, beheading the prisoner, and cutting his body in four pieces. The body pieces were then put on display in various parts of the country as a means of deterring treasonous behavior.

Breaking on the Wheel

France employed similarly cruel methods of execution, such as burning at the stake, or "breaking on the wheel." Breaking the prisoner on the wheel involved fastening the prisoner to a large wheel with their limbs stretched out along the spokes over two wooden beams. The wheel would slowly turn and an iron bar would break the prisoner's bones as his limbs passed over the beams. If the prisoner was not shown mercy, by strangling or otherwise causing his immediate death, it could take days for the prisoner to die on the wheel. The wheel would then be placed on the top of a tall pole so that birds could eat the prisoner, even if he was still alive. In a move towards more "humane" methods of execution, France developed the guillotine, which was viewed as delivering a relatively quick and painless death.

PRESENT-DAY METHODS OF EXECUTION

In General

Most states use lethal injection as their sole or primary manner of execution. The number of states authorizing lethal injection increased from 17 in 1986 to 37 in 2007.

Nevertheless, as discussed below, in addition to lethal injection, a number of states still provide for execution by hanging; firing squad; electrocution; and lethal gas. In a few jurisdictions the prisoner is allowed to choose which method of execution he or she prefers. Ironically, most death certificates issued after a prisoner is executed lists homicide as their cause of death.

Since the death penalty was reinstated in 1976, 1,099 convicted murderers have been executed in the United States, as of October 1, 2007. Of those executed: 929 (85%) were executed by lethal injection, including 443 of the last 448 executions. In addition, 154 prisoners were executed by electric chair; 11 were executed by gas chamber; 3 were executed by hanging; and 2 were executed by firing squad.

A table setting forth authorized execution methods, categorized by state, may be found in Appendix 10 of this Almanac, and a table setting forth the total number of executions conducted from 1976 through 2007, categorized by state and the methods of execution, may be found in Appendix 11 of this Almanac.

Hanging

Hanging was the traditional method of execution in the United States until the 1890s. Prior to the actual execution, a rehearsal is held using a sandbag that weighs the same as the prisoner. This is important in order to determine the length of rope needed to make sure the execution is carried out in a humane and speedy manner. At the time of execution, the prisoner is blindfolded and his or her hands and legs are bound. The noose is placed around the prisoner's neck and a trap door opens through which the prisoner falls, causing a neck fracture.

There are many drawbacks to this method of execution. For example, if the drop is too short, the noose is in the wrong position, or the inmate has very strong neck muscles, the anticipated neck fracture will not occur quickly enough, and there will be a slow and agonizing death by strangulation. If the drop is too long, there is a risk of decapitation.

Delaware, New Hampshire, and Washington still authorize hanging as a method of execution.

Delaware authorizes lethal injection for those whose capital offense occurred on or after June 13, 1986; those who committed the offense before that date may select lethal injection or hanging.

New Hampshire authorizes hanging only if lethal injection cannot be given.

The last prisoner executed by hanging was Billy Bailey in Delaware on January 25, 1996.

Firing Squad

In carrying out this method of execution, the prisoner is generally strapped into a chair in front of a canvas wall, and a hood is placed over his or her head. A target is pinned to the prisoner's chest over his or her heart. There is usually a minimum of five marksmen who stand 20 feet away in an enclosure. They are provided with loaded weapons except for one that is filled with blanks. None of the marksmen know which gun contains the blanks.

On orders, they aim their rifle at the target through a slot in the canvas and fire. The prisoner loses consciousness and quickly goes into shock due to blood loss to the brain caused by the ruptured heart or blood vessel. One drawback to this method of execution occurs if the marksmen miss the target, in which the inmate slowly bleeds to death.

Idaho, Oklahoma and Utah still authorize the firing squad as a method of execution.

Oklahoma authorizes electrocution if lethal injection is held to be unconstitutional, and firing squad if both lethal injection and electrocution are held to be unconstitutional.

Utah authorizes the firing squad if lethal injection is held unconstitutional. Inmates who selected execution by firing squad prior to May 3, 2004, may still be entitled to execution by that method.

The last prisoner executed by a firing squad was John Albert Taylor in Utah on January 26, 1996.

Electrocution

Throughout the twentieth century, electrocution was the most widely employed method of execution in the United States, purportedly as a more humane alternative to hanging. In carrying out this method of execution, the prisoner is taken into the electrocution chamber, strapped into a chair, and blindfolded. Electrodes are fastened to the prisoner's head and legs. A switch is tripped which sends a jolt of electricity between 500 and 2000 volts throughout the prisoner's body for approximately 30 seconds. A doctor checks the prisoner for a heartbeat. If a heartbeat is detected, the process is repeated.

There has been much criticism over this method of execution, particularly after one prisoner's death was reportedly prolonged by as much as 14 minutes, during which he literally caught on fire (the 1983 execution of John Evans in Alabama).

Alabama, Arkansas, Florida, Kentucky, Oklahoma, South Carolina, Tennessee and Virginia still authorize electrocution as a method of execution.

Arkansas authorizes lethal injection for those whose offense occurred on or after July 4, 1983; inmates whose offense occurred before that date may select lethal injection or electrocution.

Kentucky authorizes lethal injection for persons sentenced on or after March 31, 1998; inmates sentenced before that date may select lethal injection or electrocution.

Oklahoma authorizes electrocution if lethal injection is held to be unconstitutional, and firing squad if both lethal injection and electrocution are held to be unconstitutional.

Tennessee authorizes lethal injection for those whose capital offense occurred after December 31, 1998; those who committed the offense before that date may select electrocution by written waiver.

The last prisoner executed by electrocution was Daryl Holton in Tennessee on September 12, 2007.

On February 8, 2008, the Nebraska Supreme Court ruled that electrocution is cruel and unusual punishment under the state's constitution.

The court found that electrocution inflicted "intense pain and agonizing suffering." The electric chair was the state's sole means of execution prior to being outlawed by this decision. Thus, although Nebraska still has the death penalty on the books, it currently has no means to carry out the punishment. With the recent U.S. Supreme Court ruling in *Baze v. Rees*, that upheld lethal injection as a constitutional method of execution, it remains to be seen whether Nebraska will adopt lethal injection or abolish the death penalty altogether.

Lethal Gas

The administration of lethal gas was an effort to improve on execution by electrocution. In carrying out this method of execution, the prisoner is also taken into an airtight chamber and strapped into a chair. A container of sulfuric acid is placed underneath the chair. The chamber is sealed, and cyanide is dropped into the acid to form a lethal gas. The prisoner ultimately dies from hypoxia, which is the loss of oxygen to the brain.

Unfortunately, there have also been reported mishaps during the administration of lethal gas. In one instance, it took almost 11 minutes for the prisoner to succumb to the lethal gas, during which time he suffered violent convulsions (the 1992 execution of Don Harding in Arizona).

In 1996, the Ninth Circuit Court of Appeals in California, where the gas chamber has been used since 1933, ruled that execution by lethal gas is a "cruel and unusual punishment." Nevertheless, Arizona, California, Missouri, and Wyoming still authorize lethal gas as a method of execution.

Arizona authorizes lethal injection for persons sentenced after November 15, 1992; inmates sentenced before that date may select lethal injection or gas.

Wyoming authorizes lethal gas if lethal injection is held to be unconstitutional.

The last prisoner executed by lethal gas was Walter LeGrand in Arizona on March 3, 1999.

Lethal Injection

Execution by lethal injection is the most recently devised method of execution. In carrying out death by lethal injection, the prisoner is strapped to a gurney and a lethal mixture of drugs is administered intravenously. Sodium thiopental is injected to sleep. Pavulon or pancuronium bromide is injected to paralyze the prisoner's muscle system and stop his or her breathing. Potassium chloride is injected to stop the prisoner's heart. The prisoner dies from respiratory and cardiac arrest while unconscious.

Most view lethal injection as the most humane and acceptable manner of execution, although it is unknowable whether the prisoner suffers pain during administration of the drugs. As the U.S. Court of Appeals pointed out, there is always the risk of a cruel and prolonged death if, for example, there is "even a slight error in dosage or administration that can leave a prisoner conscious but paralyzed while dying, a sentient witness of his or her own asphyxiation." (*Chaney v. Heckler*, 718 F.2d 1174, 1983).

There have been documented problems with lethal injection. In 2007, an execution in Ohio was delayed 90 minutes as medical workers struggled to find a vein in the prisoner's arm into which they could insert the shunts to carry the intravenous lines.

Baze v. Rees

On September 25, 2007, the U.S. Supreme Court agreed to hear a Kentucky case challenging the use of lethal injection. In *Baze v. Rees*, (Docket No. 07-5439, 2005-SC-0543, 217 SW3d 207) the Supreme Court considered whether lethal injection constitutes cruel and unusual punishment as it is currently implemented. Under the court's death penalty precedents, a method of execution must not be "contrary to evolving standards of decency," and may not inflict "unnecessary pain."

In rejecting the challenge to lethal injection last year, the Kentucky Supreme Court found that the method did not present a "substantial" risk of pain and suffering, and so met the constitutional standards. The court held that: "the prohibition is against cruel punishment and does not require a complete absence of pain."

At issue in the case is was whether the most commonly used drug "cocktail" used to execute prisoners on death row is so likely to produce needless pain and suffering as to be unconstitutional, in violation of the Eighth Amendment prohibition against cruel and unusual punishment.

The appellants, Ralph Baze and Thomas Bowling, argued that a paralyzing drug can leave an inadequately anesthetized inmate with the ability to feel severe pain as another drug stops the heart, but without the ability to move or call for help. They further argued that the Kentucky court failed to consider that the risk of pain was "unnecessary," in that alternative methods of lethal injection could eliminate the chance that inmates would remain conscious but paralyzed. They urged the Court to incorporate "unnecessary risk" into the standard for evaluating lethal injection.

Appellants argued that Pavulon—the drug that paralyzes the prisoner's muscle system and stops his or her breathing—could be eliminated, and that a less painful drug could be substituted for potassium chloride, the last drug to be administered to the prisoner, which stops his or her heart.

The Kentucky attorney general's office, in urging the Court to turn down the appeal, argued that the fact that the three chemicals were so widely used demonstrated that the protocol was acceptable.

No executions had been carried out since the Supreme Court agreed to consider this issue. The case was argued by both sides before the U.S. Supreme Court on January 7, 2008, and on April 16, 2008, the Court upheld the constitutionality of lethal injection as a method of execution.

THE ROLE OF THE EXECUTIONER

In general, an execution may be carried out by prison staff, law enforcement officers, an officer of the court or, in the case of a military execution, military personnel. The executioner carries out the execution under the authority of a death warrant issued by the court.

Although doctors are called upon to certify death, e.g., by checking for a prisoner's heartbeat, a doctor is not permitted to participate in an execution.

VIEWING THE EXECUTION

In General

Executions in the United States were once carried out in the public square, before a crowd of people. Thousands of people would attend public executions and, in some instances, an admission fee was charged. The last public execution on record was a hanging that took place in Kentucky in 1936. In the late 19th century, states began to outlaw public executions. Today, executions are no longer public, and only certain interested parties are permitted to view the execution.

State laws vary as to those persons who are permitted to view an execution, but generally include: (1) victim survivors; (2) the murder victim's relatives; (3) the prisoner's relatives; (4) minister, priest, or other spiritual advisor; (5) certain medical personnel; (6) members of the media; (7) the prison warden and guards; and (8) any other state-authorized witnesses.

Once the death warrant has been signed, the witnesses are notified as to the date and time the execution will be held. If there is a stay of execution, the witnesses are also notified.

Witnesses are located in a room adjacent to the execution chamber. They are able to view the execution through a window. In some states, the window is a one-way mirror so that the prisoner is unable to see the witnesses. A witness has the right to decide not to witness the execution up until the moment of entering the execution chamber viewing area.

Victim Witnesses

Some states limit the number of victim witnesses who are eligible to view the execution, or have other eligibility restrictions:

1. Delaware—Relatives of both the victim and the condemned prisoner are allowed to witness the execution. Friends are not allowed. The prison warden and Department of Corrections officials have discretion over who may witness an execution.

2. Georgia—Allows two victim witnesses to view the execution.

3. Illinois—Allows victim witnesses to view the execution through closed circuit television only.

4. New Hampshire—Has no rules in place regarding victim witnesses.

5. North Carolina—Allows two members of the victim's family to view the execution.

6. Oregon—Allows the immediate family of victim to view the execution, including the parents, spouse, siblings, children, and grandparents of the victim, including step relationships.

7. Pennsylvania—Allows four victim witnesses to view the execution, who must be at least 21 years old.

8. South Carolina—Allows three witnesses from the victim's family to view the execution. If there is more than one victim, the number of family representatives may be reduced to one for each victim family. If there are more than two victims, the total number of victims' representatives present may be restricted in accordance with the space limitation of the facility.

9. Texas—Allows five victim witnesses to view the execution.

10. Washington—The number of victim witnesses who are allowed to view the execution is determined by the superintendent.

CHAPTER 3:
THE FEDERAL DEATH PENALTY

IN GENERAL

In addition to state capital punishment laws, the federal government also employs the death penalty for certain federal offenses. The first execution under the federal death penalty was carried out on June 25, 1790 in Maine.

The federal death penalty differs from the death penalty at the state level in that the federal death penalty encompasses a variety of crimes beyond that of first-degree murder, including terrorism and large-scale drug trafficking. The federal death penalty can also be applied within any state whether or not it has the death penalty.

Between 1790 and 1963, the federal government executed 340 prisoners, including 4 women. The crimes that led to these executions included murder, rape, kidnapping, rioting, piracy, and espionage. Thirty-four of these executions, which included 2 women, were held between 1927 and 1963.

There were no federal executions after the 1963 hanging of Victor Feguer in Iowa for kidnapping until the death penalty was reinstated in 1988. When the 1972 Supreme Court ruling in *Furman*, declared the state death penalty statutes unconstitutional, the older federal death penalty statutes were similarly found to be arbitrary and capricious.

The federal government subsequently enacted a number of new statutes authorizing the death penalty. Between 1994 and 2005, there were 48 executions pursuant to these statutes.

A table of federal capital offenses, by statute may be found in Appendix 7 of this Almanac.

METHODS OF EXECUTION

In carrying out the 340 executions that took place before 1963, the federal government used hanging, electrocution, and lethal gas.

Under the 1988 federal death penalty law, there was no particular method of execution set forth in the statute. In 1993, regulations were issued by President Bush that authorized lethal injection as the method of execution under federal law.

Nevertheless, the 1994 expanded death penalty law provides that the manner of execution will be the method employed by the state in which the federal sentence is handed down. If the particular state is a non-death penalty state, then the presiding judge is authorized to choose another state for carrying out the death sentence.

THE ANTI-DRUG ABUSE ACT OF 1988 (THE "DRUG KINGPIN" STATUTE)

In 1988, a new federal death penalty statute was enacted for murders committed in the course of a "drug kingpin" conspiracy. The Anti-Drug Abuse Act authorizes the death penalty for a defendant convicted in federal court of a murder committed while engaging in a continuing criminal enterprise. This federal statute was carefully modeled after the state statutes that received approval from the Supreme Court following the 1972 decision in *Furman*.

The Act requires the government to prove beyond a reasonable doubt that the defendant intended to commit the murder and that certain aggravating factors applied to the offense. The jury must be unanimous in finding that an aggravating factor exists. The Act also permits the defendant to present evidence of any mitigating factors for the jury's consideration.

The jurors are not required to be unanimous in their findings as to mitigating factors. They are required, however, to weigh the aggravating and mitigating factors against each other before deciding whether or not to impose a death sentence. Nevertheless, the jurors are not required to recommend a death sentence even if they find that the aggravating factors outweigh the mitigating factors.

Juan Raul Garza was the first person to be executed under the federal Anti-Drug Abuse Act, which imposes a death sentence for murders stemming from a drug enterprise. On August 10, 1993, Garza was convicted of various marijuana drug trafficking laws, money laundering, and three counts of murder in furtherance of a "continuing criminal enterprise." He was executed on June 19, 2001 by lethal injection at the federal prison in Terre Haute, Indiana.

THE FEDERAL DEATH PENALTY ACT OF 1994
(THE "CRIME BILL EXPANSION")

The federal death penalty was used sparingly up until the mid 20th Century, and not at all from 1972 until the adoption of the Anti-Drug Abuse Act in 1988. With the Federal Death Penalty Act of 1994, the scope of the federal death penalty further broadened. As part of an omnibus crime bill, the federal death penalty was expanded to include approximately 60 different offenses. Included in the federal statutes authorizing a sentence of death are espionage; treason; genocide; and the following murder-related crimes:

1. Murder related to the smuggling of aliens;

2. Murder committed during a drug-related drive-by shooting;

3. Murder committed at an airport serving international civil aviation;

4. Retaliatory murder of a member of the immediate family of law enforcement officials;

5. Murder of a member of Congress, an important executive official, or a Supreme Court Justice;

6. Murder committed by the use of a firearm during a crime of violence or drug-trafficking crime;

7. Murder committed in a federal government facility;

8. First-degree murder; murder of a federal judge or law enforcement official;

9. Murder of a foreign official;

10. Murder by a federal prisoner;

11. Murder of a U.S. national in a foreign country;

12. Murder of a state or local law enforcement official or other person aiding in a federal investigation;

13. Murder of a state correctional officer;

14. Murder during a kidnapping;

15. Murder during a hostage taking;

16. Murder of a court officer or juror;

17. Murder with the intent of preventing testimony by a witness, victim or informant; retaliatory murder of a witness, victim, or informant;

18. Murder for hire;

19. Murder involved in a racketeering offense;

20. Murder related to a bank robbery or kidnapping;

21. Murder related to a carjacking;

22. Murder related to rape or child molestation;

23. Murder related to sexual exploitation of children;

24. Murder committed during an offense against maritime navigation;

25. Terrorist murder of a U.S. national in another country;

26. Murder by the use of a weapon of mass destruction;

27. Murder involving torture; and

28. Murder related to a continuing criminal enterprise or related murder of a federal, state, or local law enforcement officer.

RACE AND THE FEDERAL DEATH PENALTY

During the 20th century, minority prisoners made up 61% of all federal executions. Of the 340 people executed between 1790 and 1963, 134 (39%) were white; 118 (35%) were black; 63 (19%) were Native American; and 25 (7%) were either Hispanic or unknown.

According to the 2000 Survey of the Federal Death Penalty System conducted by the Department of Justice (DOJ), there were numerous racial disparities in the way the death penalty was assessed. Between 1988 and 1994, 5 prisoners were under sentence of death, of which 1 (20%) was white; 3 (60%) were black; and 1 (20%) was Hispanic. Between 1995 and 2000, 14 prisoners were under sentence of death, of which 3 (21.4%) were white; 10 (71.4%) were black; and 1 (7.1%) was listed as "other."

The DOJ survey also found that 80% of the cases submitted by federal prosecutors for death penalty review between 1995 and 2000 involved racial minorities as defendants and, in more than half of those cases, the defendants were black.

Since 1988, the federal government has authorized seeking the death penalty against 382 defendants. Of the 382 approved prosecutions, 278 (73%) were against minority defendants. Of these defendants, 104 were white, 195 were black, 64 were Hispanic, 16 were Asian/Indian/Pacific Islander, and 3 were Arab. Of the 44 inmates currently on federal death row, 26 (59%) are members of a minority group.

PROCEDURE

Authorization

In a federal death penalty case, the local United States Attorney's Office must obtain the written consent of the Attorney General before seeking the death penalty. The Department of Justice reviews each case and gives its recommendation to the Attorney General. Attorneys for the defense are allowed to present reasons why the death penalty should not be sought. The Attorney General makes the final decision on whether or not to authorize the death penalty.

Right to Legal Representation

If a prisoner is indicted for a federal capital crime and is unable to afford legal representation, he or she will be assigned two defense attorneys. One of these attorneys must be "learned in the law of capital cases" and meet the minimum standards for attorneys appointed in capital cases. Because a federal capital case is complex, the assistance of a competent and experienced lawyer is crucial.

Appeal

As set forth in Chapter 8, Sentence Review, in a federal death penalty case, there is only one appeal granted to a defendant as a matter of right—an appeal of the sentence and conviction to the U.S. Court of Appeals for the Circuit in which the case was tried. The defendant may seek a reversal of his or her conviction or sentence if it was caused by any legal errors during the trial.

If the appellant is unsuccessful, he or she has one additional chance to present any facts or evidence that may have been unavailable, neglected or concealed at trial, or certain claims of constitutional error that could not have been raised on appeal.

All other review, such as U.S. Supreme Court review, is on a discretionary basis, and can only be requested once. An exception may exist in an extraordinary case where clear proof of innocence exists, or blatant constitutional violations occurred.

Clemency

A federal death row prisoner is given 120 days' notice of his or her execution date, and has 30 days to file a clemency petition once the execution date has been set. The United States President is the only one who has the power to pardon a federal death row prisoner.

COSTS

Prosecution

According to a 1998 report by the Subcommittee on Federal Death Penalty Cases, the average total cost of prosecuting an authorized federal death penalty case, not including non-attorney investigative costs or the costs of experts and other assistance provided by law enforcement agencies was $365,000.

Defense

According to the 1998 Subcommittee report, the costs of defending a case in which the Attorney General decides to seek the death penalty for a capital offense is much higher than the cost of defending a case in which the Attorney General declines to authorize the death penalty.

For example, the average total cost per representation of a sample of cases in which the defendant was charged with an offense punishable by death and the Attorney General authorized seeking the death penalty was $218,112. On the other hand, the average total cost per representation of a sample of cases in which the defendant was charged with an offense punishable by death and the Attorney General did not authorize seeking the death penalty was $55,772.

In addition, the cost of defending a federal death penalty case that is resolved by means of a trial is higher than the cost of defending a case that is resolved through a guilty plea, even though many guilty pleas are entered after most of the preparation for trial has been completed.

For example, the total cost per representation of a sample of authorized federal death penalty cases resolved through a guilty plea was $192,333; whereas the total cost per representation of a sample of authorized federal death penalty cases resolved through a trial was $269,139.

NATIVE AMERICANS

The use of the federal death penalty on Native American reservations has been left to the discretion of the tribal governments. Almost all the tribes have chosen not to use the federal death penalty.

U.S. MILITARY

History

The U.S. military has its own death penalty statute, under which prisoners have been executed since 1916. However, there have been no military executions for over 35 years. The last execution was carried out on April 13, 1961. Private John Bennett was convicted of rape and attempted murder, and hanged at Fort Leavenworth in Kansas.

In 1983, the Armed Forces Court of Appeals held that military capital sentencing procedures were unconstitutional for failing to require a finding of individualized aggravating circumstances *(U.S. v. Matthews,* 16 M.J. 354 (1983)).

In 1984, the death penalty was reinstated when President Reagan signed an executive order adopting detailed rules for a capital court martial. Among the rules was a list of 11 aggravating factors that qualify defendants for death sentences. The Uniform Code of Military Justice provides the death penalty as a possible punishment for 15 offenses (10 USC Sections 886–934), many of which must occur during a time of war.

An amendment to the Uniform Code of Military Justice provides for an alternative to the death penalty. For crimes that occurred on or after November 17, 1997, a sentence of life without the possibility of parole is available.

Demographics

According to a March 2008 study by the Federal Death Penalty Resource Counsel, since 1984, there have been 47 capital courts-martial resulting in 15 death sentences. As of January 1, 2007, 9 military prisoners were on death row, of which 2 are white; 6 are black; and 1 is Asian. All of the prisoners are male. The minimum age under the U.S. Military death penalty statute is 18 years old.

Prosecution

In a military capital case, the convening authority that decides to bring the case to a court martial also decides if the death penalty will be sought. The convening authority then chooses those service members who will serve as panel members, i.e., jurors. The panel must consist of at least five members. If the accused so chooses, at least one-third of the panel must consist of enlisted personnel.

Only the United States President can approve and order the execution of a death sentence. The President has the power to commute a death sentence, thus no service member can be executed unless the President personally confirms the death penalty.

Once the President approves the sentence, the Secretary of the Army is responsible for providing the initial notification of the President's approval of the death sentence via the Provost Marshal General to the Commandant of the United States Disciplinary Barracks.

Following is a sample Notification Letter:

On [Date], The President of the United States approved the sentence, including the sentence to death in [United States v. Full Name of Prisoner] in accordance with Article 71(c)(1), Uniform Code of Military Justice.

Secretary of the Army

Signature

The Secretary of the Army is also responsible for approving the location for the execution, and setting the date of the execution. However, the execution date can be no sooner than 60 days from the date the President approves the death sentence.

The Provost Marshal General is responsible for providing the signed execution order of the President's approval of the death sentence through the Commanding General, U.S. Army Training and Doctrine Command, to the Commandant of the United States Disciplinary Barracks. This notification must be made as soon as possible, but not before the initial notification to the condemned prisoner.

Following is a sample Execution Order:

MEMORANDUM THRU Provost Marshal General, 2800 Army Pentagon, Washington, DC 20310-2800

FOR Commandant, United States Disciplinary Barracks

1. On [Date], The President of the United States approved the sentence, including the sentence to death in [United States v. Name of Prisoner] on [Date/Time of Execution] by lethal injection, in accordance with AR 190-55.
2. The execution officer will be the Commandant, United States Disciplinary Barracks.

Secretary of the Army

Signature/Date/Time

The U.S. Disciplinary Barracks

The United States Disciplinary Barracks (USDB) is a military prison located at Fort Leavenworth, a United States Army Post in Kansas. It is the oldest penal institution in continuous operation in the federal system.

The USDB is a maximum-security facility that houses male service members who have been convicted at court-martial for violations of the Uniform Code of Military Justice (UCMJ). The UCMJ is the foundation of military law, and applies to all members of the United States Uniformed Services.

Prisoners housed in the USDB include commissioned officers, enlisted prisoners with sentences over 7 years, and prisoners who have been convicted of offenses related to national security, including prisoners who have been sentenced to death.

Execution Procedure

In January 2006, the U.S. Military issued new regulations regarding executions (U.S. Army Regulation 190-55). The regulations prescribe policies and procedures for carrying out death sentences imposed by military courts–martial or military tribunals and approved by the President of the United States, whose order is necessary to approve the execution of a death sentence.

Under the new regulations, the execution procedure is as follows:

1. The execution is conducted by means of continuous intravenous administration of a lethal substance, or substances, in a quantity sufficient to cause death.

2. The condemned prisoner will be moved from his cell to the execution area prior to the execution with a time duration limited to the minimum amount of time absolutely necessary to prepare the prisoner for execution.

3. The condemned prisoner will be placed on the execution table and restrained by means of appropriate fasteners to ensure safety and security of the prisoner and the execution watch team personnel. The execution watch team consists of personnel who are specifically trained and medically certified, and are responsible for the actual conduct of the execution by lethal injection.

4. Once the prisoner is secured to the table, the execution team will insert a large–bore intravenous channel into an appropriate vein, assure the flow of a normal saline solution, and connect the condemned prisoner to the electrocardiograph machine.

5. The execution area will be cleared of all nonessential personnel. At that time, the execution area will be opened and made visible to all assembled witnesses.

6. Those personnel approved to witness the execution will be escorted from the witness assembly area to the witness viewing rooms prior to the opening of the execution area.

7. Witnesses arriving after others have been escorted to the witness viewing rooms will normally not be permitted to enter or view the execution.

8. Once in the viewing area, all witnesses will receive a final briefing on the specifics of the procedure they are about to observe and the behavior and decorum expected. Those who cannot maintain the expected level of behavior will be removed.

9. At no time will media representatives conduct interviews of witnesses while congregated in the witness assembly or viewing areas.

10. At the time designated for the execution, the Commandant of the U.S. Disciplinary Barracks will read aloud the charge or charges, the finding of the court, the sentence, and the execution orders. The Commandant will then order the execution to begin.

11. Following the Commandant's reading of the documents listed above, the execution team will administer the lethal agents.

12. The execution team will monitor vital signs and notify the Commandant when no vital signs remain.

13. The Commandant will then announce that the execution is completed.

14. At that time all persons, including the witnesses, will leave the viewing area, except those designated members of the execution watch team responsible for removal of the body.

15. A senior medical officer, appointed by the Surgeon General, will certify death and provide a report of death at the morgue or medical facility.

16. The senior medical officer will notify the Fort Leavenworth Casualty Office of the prisoner's death.

17. Persons authorized to direct disposition may designate the Army to provide the mortuary benefits.

Authorized Witnesses

According to the 2006 regulations, the following individuals and representatives are authorized to be present at the execution:

1. The Commandant of the United States Disciplinary Barracks (USDB);

2. A representative from the Provost Marshall General;

3. The USDB cadre, as deemed appropriate by the Commandant, for security purposes and to ensure professional military conduct of the execution;

4. Contracted execution team members;

5. The prisoner's counsel of record, if requested by the condemned prisoner;

6. A chaplain designated by the Commandant, or at the request of the prisoner, including contracted civilian clergy support;

7. A minimum of 2 media representatives, selected from a pool of media representatives requesting to witness the execution; and

8. Representatives of the condemned prisoner's family, if requested by the prisoner.

CHAPTER 4:
LEGAL REPRESENTATION

IN GENERAL

It is often argued that the lack of adequate legal representation for indigent defendants facing the death penalty justifies abolition of capital punishment. In fact, the quality of a defendant's legal representation is arguably the determining factor in whether the defendant receives the death penalty.

Approximately 90% of the prisoners facing execution on capital offenses cannot afford their own lawyer. Their fate is literally in the hands of an attorney who is assigned to represent the defendant for little or no compensation. Many public defenders carry an enormous caseload and simply cannot give the proper attention that each case deserves. Others lack the requisite experience necessary to present an adequate defense in a capital case.

STATISTICS

As set forth below, according to the Bureau of Justice Statistics, the majority of prisoners—state, federal, and local—are represented by some type of assigned counsel.

State Prisoners

Ninety-seven percent of state prisoners reported that they were represented by an attorney. Seventy-six percent of those who had legal counsel indicated that they were represented by a public defender or assigned counsel in connection with the offense for which they were now serving time. Among those represented by legal counsel, 79% of blacks and 73% of whites reported representation by an assigned attorney.

Federal Prisoners

Ninety-nine percent of federal prisoners reported that they were represented by an attorney. Forty-three percent of those prisoners were represented by private counsel, which accounted for nearly 50% of white prisoners and 33% of black prisoners. The remaining federal prisoners—over 50%—were represented by a public defender or assigned counsel in connection with the offense for which they were now serving time.

Local Prisoners

Eighty-three percent of local jail inmates reported that they were represented by an attorney. Approximately 75% of those prisoners who had legal counsel indicated that they were represented by a public defender or assigned counsel in connection with the offense for which they were now serving time.

QUALIFICATIONS AND COMPETENCY

Some individuals may be fortunate enough to be assigned a lawyer who is relatively competent, and who has some experience in handling death penalty cases. However, more often than not, the attorney assigned to represent an indigent defendant facing the death penalty has little or no experience with capital offense cases, and may even be a recent law school graduate.

Although many assigned attorneys are dedicated to their client's case, there have been complaints that some assigned attorneys are so disinterested in these low or non-paying assigned cases, that they do not take the required time or make the necessary efforts to adequately represent the client.

Even worse, there are reported instances where attorneys assigned to death penalty cases have engaged in the following incompetent or unethical behaviors:

1. Failed to appear in court;

2. Appeared intoxicated in court;

3. Fallen asleep during the trial; and

4. Failed to make critical motions or obtain important exculpatory evidence that could have proven their client's innocence.

Nevertheless, even if the defense attorney has the necessary skills, and is dedicated to providing the client with the best representation, he or she is generally without the financial resources necessary to conduct an adequate investigation and defense. In addition, assigned defense attorneys usually handle a large caseload and cannot expend all of their energy on any one client's defense.

The widely broadcast "O.J. Simpson trial" demonstrated that the ability to retain expensive attorneys, experts and investigators could mean the difference between a conviction and an acquittal. Unfortunately, the indigent defendant can never realistically expect to receive this kind of defense.

Providing the indigent defendant with an attorney who is fairly compensated, and further providing that attorney with the funds and resources necessary to conduct a thorough defense, is not a government or taxpayer priority. The result is that defendants who are unable to pay for the best defense are more likely to receive inadequate representation, and more likely to find themselves on death row facing execution.

Despite the Supreme Court's post-*Furman* approval of revised state capital punishment statutes, application of the death penalty based on financial resources results in an unfair and arbitrary outcome, which still disproportionately targets the poor, the less educated, and members of minority groups.

U.S. SUPREME COURT CASES

The following U.S. Supreme Court cases highlight the issue of inadequate defense in capital cases:

Strickland v. Washington

In *Strickland v. Washington*, 466 U.S. 668 (1984), the defendant appealed his death sentence arguing that he received ineffective assistance of counsel at sentencing because his attorney failed to request a psychiatric report, to investigate and present character witnesses, and to seek a presentence report.

After a number of unsuccessful appeals at the lower court levels, the Court of Appeals ultimately reversed, stating that, under the Sixth Amendment, criminal defendants had the right to reasonably effective assistance of counsel. After outlining standards for judging whether the defense counsel fulfilled the duty to investigate nonstatutory mitigating circumstances and whether counsel's errors were sufficiently prejudicial to justify reversal, the Court of Appeals remanded the case for application of the standards.

On remand, the U.S. Supreme Court reversed the Court of Appeals ruling, and set forth a two-prong test. The Court ruled that a convicted defendant's claim that counsel's assistance was so defective as to require reversal of a conviction, or setting aside of a death sentence, requires that the defendant show: (1) that counsel's performance was deficient; and (2) that the deficient performance prejudiced the defense so as to deprive the defendant of a fair trial.

Deficient Performance of Counsel

The proper standard for judging attorney performance is that of reasonably effective assistance, considering all the circumstances. When a convicted defendant complains of the ineffectiveness of counsel's assistance, the defendant must show that counsel's representation fell below an objective standard of reasonableness.

Judicial scrutiny of counsel's performance must be highly deferential, and a fair assessment of attorney performance requires that every effort be made to eliminate the distorting effects of hindsight, to reconstruct the circumstances of counsel's challenged conduct, and to evaluate the conduct from counsel's perspective at the time. A court must indulge a strong presumption that counsel's conduct falls within the wide range of reasonable professional assistance. These standards require no special amplification in order to define counsel's duty to investigate.

Deficient Performance Prejudiced Defendant's Right to Fair Trial

With regard to the required showing of prejudice, the proper standard requires the defendant to show that there is a reasonable probability that, but for counsel's unprofessional errors, the result of the proceeding would have been different. A reasonable probability is a probability sufficient to undermine confidence in the outcome. A court hearing an ineffectiveness claim must consider the totality of the evidence before the judge or jury.

Further, a court need not first determine whether counsel's performance was deficient before examining the prejudice suffered by the defendant as a result of the alleged deficiencies. If it is easier to dispose of an ineffectiveness claim on the ground of lack of sufficient prejudice, that course should be followed.

Williams v. Taylor

In *Williams v. Taylor*, Docket No. 98-8384 (2000), in a 6-3 decision, the U.S. Supreme Court held that the Virginia Supreme Court applied the wrong test when examining a claim that Williams' lawyer was ineffective in the sentencing phase of his trial. The Court also disagreed with the U.S. Court of Appeals for the Fourth Circuit, which had upheld Williams' death sentence. Williams' lawyer had failed to present evidence of child abuse, borderline mental retardation, and potential for reform in his client's history. The Court held that such information might well have led to a different sentence.

Cockrell v. Burdine

In *Cockrell v. Burdine*, Docket No. 01-495 (2002), the U.S. Supreme Court declined to decide an appeal by the State of Texas of a Fifth Circuit Court ruling that granted Texas death row inmate Calvin Burdine a new trial on the basis of ineffective counsel. According to several witnesses, Burdine's attorney dozed repeatedly during his original trial. The Circuit Court held that "unconscious counsel equates to no counsel at all," and that Burdine was therefore "denied counsel at a critical stage of his trial."

Bell v. Cone

In *Bell v. Cone*, Docket No. 01-400 (2002), in an 8-1 decision, the U.S. Supreme Court upheld the death sentence of Gary Cone from Tennessee, despite the fact that his lawyer presented no mitigating evidence on Cone's behalf and passed up an opportunity to argue for his life. The attorney was reportedly suffering from mental illness and later committed suicide.

The Court ruled that the attorney's inaction did not amount to a complete absence of representation, and that the state court did not act unreasonably when it held that the attorney might have been making a tactical decision in not presenting evidence.

Wiggins v. Smith

In *Wiggins v. Smith*, Docket No. 02-311 (2003), in a 7-2 decision, the United States Supreme Court reversed and remanded the sentence of Maryland death row inmate Kevin Wiggins on the basis of inadequate representation by his original trial attorneys. Standard procedure in Maryland at the time of the trial included preparation of a "social history" report that would contain mitigation investigations regarding the case.

As no such report was prepared or even requested, Justice O'Connor, writing for the court, remarked that "[a]ny reasonably competent attorney would have realized that pursuing such leads was necessary to making an informed choice among possible defenses, particularly given the apparent absence of aggravating factors from Wiggins' background." Wiggins' original lawyers made no attempt to inform members of the jury that sent Wiggins to death row that their client was repeatedly raped, beaten and denied food as a child, and that his mother burned his hands on the stove as punishment. The Court concluded that the "performance of Wiggins' attorneys at sentencing violated his Sixth Amendment right to effective assistance of counsel."

Florida v. Nixon

In *Florida v. Nixon*, Docket No. 03-391 (2004), the U.S. Supreme Court ruled that the effectiveness of defense counsel's performance must be judged by standards previously set out by the Court in *Strickland v. Washington*. Joe Nixon's attorney told the jury his client was guilty without his client's express consent. After the jury sentenced Nixon to death, the Florida Supreme Court overturned Nixon's conviction, holding that counsel's concession of guilt automatically fell below an objective standard of reasonable performance, necessitating a new trial. The court ruled that counsel's performance was deficient and that the deficient performance was presumptively prejudicial to Nixon.

The U.S. Supreme Court overruled the Florida court, holding that a concession of guilt by counsel made without the express consent of the defendant does not automatically constitute ineffective assistance of counsel, but must be judged by *Strickland's* two-pronged test: sub-par representation and a likely effect on the outcome of the case.

Rompilla v. Beard

In *Rompilla v. Beard*, Docket No. 04-5462 (2005), in a 5-4 decision, the Supreme Court granted habeas relief and ordered a new sentencing trial for Pennsylvania death row inmate Ronald Rompilla after finding that his trial counsel failed to meet the standard of reasonable competence under *Strickland v. Washington*. The Court held that the state court's resolution of Rompilla's ineffective-assistance of counsel claim resulted in a decision that "involved an unreasonable application of clearly established Federal law."

The Court noted that Rompilla's trial attorney failed to investigate records showing possible mitigating evidence of mental retardation and a traumatic upbringing, even after prosecutors gave warning they planned to use the same documents against Rompilla. The Court ruled that even when a capital defendant's family members and the defendant himself have suggested that no mitigating evidence is available, his lawyer is bound to make reasonable efforts to obtain and review material that counsel knows the prosecution will probably rely on as evidence of aggravation at the sentencing phase of trial. The Court stated that the undiscovered mitigating evidence, taken as a whole, "might well have influenced the jury's appraisal."

THE ADOPTION OF STANDARDS

In an effort to provide indigent defendants with a better chance at fair representation, particularly in death penalty cases, a number of states have adopted standards of qualifications for the representation of indigent defendants. For example:

Alabama

Alabama requires that an attorney assigned to a capital case have no less than five years prior experience in the active practice of criminal law.

Nevada

Nevada requires that the assigned attorney shall have had experience defending no less than seven felony trials, at least two of which involved violent crimes, including at least one murder case.

Texas

The Texas Criminal Court of Appeals adopted new rules that will set standards for criminal representation and remove attorneys whose work "falls below professional standards." The new rules enforce the 11-year-old state law that guarantees death row inmates competent legal assistance in filing appeals.

Utah

Utah requires that counsel for an indigent defendant in a capital case must have tried to verdict six felony cases within the past four years or twenty-five felony cases total, five of which must have been tried to verdict within the past five years. In addition, at least one of the attorneys must have appeared as counsel or co-counsel in a capital homicide case which was tried to a jury and which went to final verdict. In addition, one of the appointed attorneys must have attended and completed within the past five years an approved continuing legal education course dealing with the trial of death penalty cases.

A table setting forth the states which have adopted standards of qualification in the legal representation of indigent defendants in capital cases, and details of their respective standards, may be found in Appendix 12 of this Almanac.

INDIGENT DEFENSE PROGRAMS

Although the Supreme Court ruled that states must provide legal counsel for indigent defendants accused of a crime, there were no specific provisions on how to implement this task. The states have thus devised their own systems for providing counsel for poor defendants.

There are three primary systems used by State and local governments to provide legal representation to indigent defendants, including: (1) the public defender program ("legal aid"); (2) the assigned counsel program; and (3) the contract attorney program.

Traditionally, assigned counsel systems and public defender programs have been the primary means to provide legal representation to the poor. Among all prosecutorial districts, a public defender program was used exclusively in 28% of the cases, an assigned counsel system in 23% of the cases, and a contract attorney system in 8% of the cases. Forty-one percent of the prosecutors' offices reported that a combination of methods was used in their jurisdiction. The most prevalent was a combination of an assigned counsel system and a public defender program.

Public Defender Programs

Public defender programs are public or private nonprofit organizations that generally employ a full or part-time staff. Local public defenders often operate autonomously. Under a statewide system, an individual is usually appointed by the governor, and charged with developing and maintaining a system of representation for each county.

In 30 states, the public defender system is the primary method used to provide legal counsel to indigent criminal defendants.

Assigned Counsel Programs

Assigned counsel programs involve the court appointment of private attorneys from a list, as the need arises. There are two types of assigned counsel programs: (1) The Ad Hoc Assigned Counsel Program; and (2) The Coordinated Assigned Counsel Program.

The Ad Hoc Assigned Counsel Program

The "Ad Hoc" assigned counsel program is one in which individual private attorneys are appointed by a judge to provide representation on a case-by-case basis.

The Coordinated Assigned Counsel Program

The "Coordinated" assigned counsel programs utilize an administrator who oversees the appointment of counsel, and develops standards and guidelines for program administration.

Contract Attorney Programs

Contract attorney programs involve agreements between governmental and bar associations, private law firms, and private attorneys, which provide legal services for indigent defendants over a specified period of time for a specific sum of money.

The Federal Indigent Defense Program

As established by the Criminal Justice Act of 1964, the federal justice system provides indigent defense to eligible defendants through private attorneys, community defender organizations, and Federal Defender Services.

CHAPTER 5:
INNOCENCE

IN GENERAL

One of the primary arguments cited by opponents of capital punishment is the risk of executing an innocent person—"wrongful execution." The death penalty is the only sentence that cannot be remedied once carried out, if subsequent proof of innocence materializes.

Although some supporters of capital punishment believe that the death penalty is necessary, despite the occasional execution of an innocent person, most argue that this scenario is unlikely. However, a number of studies undertaken since the 1980s have demonstrated that innocent people are convicted of capital crimes, and that some have been executed before they could introduce evidence of their innocence.

The American Bar Association (ABA) has conducted a number of studies concerning innocence and the administration of the death penalty. According to its research, numerous, critical flaws in current practices, coupled with the federal habeas law and federal defunding of the death penalty resource centers, have compounded the problem of the conviction of innocent people. The ABA has concluded that executions must stop unless and until greater fairness and due process can be assured in death penalty administration.

The Innocence Project is a national litigation and public policy organization dedicated to exonerating wrongfully convicted people through DNA testing, and reforming the criminal justice system to prevent such future injustices.

WRONGFUL CONVICTION AND EXECUTION

Wrongful conviction occurs when an individual is convicted and punished for a crime that he or she did not commit. Wrongful execution occurs when that individual is sentenced to death and subsequently executed for the capital crime he or she did not commit.

Contributing Factors

The following factors reportedly contribute to the risk that innocent individuals will be wrongfully convicted and sentenced to death:

Expansion of Capital Crimes

There has been an expansion in the number of state and federal crimes leading to death sentences. In addition, more states have added the death penalty. More death sentences necessarily lead to more convictions of innocent defendants.

Juror Bias

For a number of reasons, jurors may start out more inclined to convict the defendant in a capital case. Death penalty cases usually involve particularly brutal and shocking evidence that alone can outrage a jury and make it more likely that they will return a guilty verdict. Further, capital crimes that receive a lot of publicity may influence jurors by introducing them to inflammatory, inadmissible and erroneous information.

During a pre-trial questioning process known as *voir dire*, jurors are generally asked about their attitudes towards the death penalty. Jurors who are against imposing a death penalty will not be chosen to serve. The result is a jury who is ready and willing to return a death sentence. A recent study of jurors in death penalty cases found that the majority of jurors formed an opinion about the defendant's sentence before hearing any evidence at the punishment phase of the trial.

Laboratory Mistakes

According to the Innocence Project, in over half of those cases where the defendant was exonerated by DNA, the misapplication of forensic discipline—such as blood type testing, hair analysis, fingerprint analysis, bite mark analysis, etc.—has played a role in convicting the innocent defendant. In these cases, forensic scientists and prosecutors presented fraudulent, exaggerated, or otherwise tainted evidence to the judge or jury that led to the wrongful conviction.

Lack of Defense Funding

There is a lack of funding for the defense of those accused of capital crimes. In order to put on an adequate defense, the attorney must have the resources to employ competent experts and investigators. This is often impossible when defending an indigent person. States have severely limited defense resources, and federal funding of the death penalty resource centers has been withdrawn.

In addition, defense lawyers must also be prepared at the outset to represent the defendant during the critical sentencing phase in the event that he or she is convicted. Thus, the attorney's time and efforts are split between getting an acquittal or preventing the client's death should he or she be convicted.

Narrowing of Appellate Rights in Capital Cases

Recent changes in the appeals process, particularly in federal courts, have made it more likely that executions will proceed despite evidence which points to a defendant's innocence. Both state and federal legislation threatens to severely shorten the length of time between conviction and execution of death row prisoners.

Currently, the average time between sentencing and execution is eight years. If that time is significantly shortened, executions will occur before there is any time to uncover evidence of innocence.

Politics

Politics play a big part in death penalty administration. Politicians and judges usually run on pro-death penalty platforms in an effort to garner public support.

In addition, prosecutors and police are under great pressure to solve the abhorrent crimes that generally constitute capital offenses, and the goal is to obtain a conviction.

Unreliable Evidence

According to the Innocence Project, unreliable evidence is the leading cause of wrongful convictions that result in an innocent person being sent to death row, as set forth below.

Mistaken Eyewitness Testimony

In the United States, mistaken eyewitness identification testimony was a factor in 77% of cases where DNA evidence exonerated the defendant post-conviction. Thus, mistaken eyewitness identification is the leading cause of these wrongful convictions.

Further, of that 77%, 48% of the cases where race was known involved cross-racial eyewitness identification. This presents an additional concern insofar as studies have shown that people are less able to recognize faces of a different race than their own, making mistaken eyewitness identification in such cases more likely.

Unreliable Witnesses

In many capital cases, such as murder, there is a lack of eyewitness evidence; therefore, the prosecution must rely on less credible types of evidence to make their case. This includes testimony from generally unreliable witnesses such as accomplices to the crime, and fellow prisoners who may testify in return for some type of deal, such as reduced or dropped charges, or special treatment.

In fact, 15% of wrongful convictions that were later overturned by DNA testing were caused in part by so-called "snitch testimony." Thus, prosecutors should be required to reveal any incentive the prisoner or accomplice might receive in return for testimony, and defense attorneys are advised to ask the judge to instruct the jury that such testimony is unreliable and was offered in return for a deal.

Unreliable Confessions

False confessions are another leading cause of wrongful convictions. Pressure by the police, or a defendant's mental illness or disability, can motivate an innocent suspect to offer false statements to satisfy the authorities. Therefore, a defendant's confession—often the primary evidence in a capital case—is not a dependable indicator of guilt.

According to statistics, 25% of wrongful conviction cases involve a false confession or incriminating statement made by the defendant. Of those cases, 35% of the defendants were 18 or under and/or developmentally disabled.

In order to prevent coercion and provide an accurate recording of interrogation proceedings, law enforcement is encouraged to record all custodial interrogations. In fact, more than 350 jurisdictions have voluntarily adopted policies to record interrogations.

DNA ACCESS LAWS

Unfortunately, even though newly discovered DNA evidence may be able to prove a defendant's innocence, some courts will not consider such evidence after the trial is over. Often, the only way a prisoner can access the DNA evidence associated with his or her criminal case is through post-conviction DNA testing access statutes. However, not all states have post-conviction DNA testing access laws.

Presently, the federal government and 43 states have post-conviction DNA testing access laws. Seven states do not allow prisoners to access DNA evidence, including: Alabama, Alaska, Massachusetts, Mississippi, Oklahoma, South Carolina, and South Dakota.

The scope of the state DNA access laws varies considerably. Some states do not permit DNA access testing if the defendant originally pled guilty to the crime. Many laws fail to include adequate safeguards for the preservation of DNA evidence. In addition, some statutory provisions make DNA access extremely difficult by placing the burden on the defense to, in effect, solve the crime and prove that the DNA evidence will implicate another individual.

The Justice For All Act of 2004

On October 30, 2004, President George W. Bush signed The Justice For All Act of 2004. The Justice For All Act includes the Innocence Protection Act, legislation that, among other things, grants any federal inmate the right to petition a federal court for DNA testing to support a claim of innocence. It also encourages states to adopt adequate measures to preserve evidence and make post-conviction DNA testing available to inmates seeking to prove their innocence.

Other key provisions of the Act include assistance to states that have the death penalty to create effective systems for the appointment and performance of qualified counsel, together with better training and monitoring for both the defense and prosecution. The Act provides substantial funding to states for increased reliance on DNA testing in new criminal investigations, and increases the amount of compensation available to wrongfully convicted federal prisoners.

Post-Conviction DNA Exonerations

According to the Innocence Project, there have been 214 post-conviction DNA exonerations in the United States in 32 states. The first DNA exoneration took place in 1989, and there have been 151 exonerations since 2000.

The average length of time the exonerated prisoners served in prison was 12 years, and 16 of those prisoners served time on death row.

The average age of the exonerated prisoners at the time they were wrongfully convicted was 26 years of age. The racial breakdown of those exonerated included 130 black prisoners; 59 white prisoners; 19 Hispanic prisoners; 1 Asian-American prisoner; and 5 prisoners of unknown racial background.

As set forth below, the concern that innocent people will be sent to their death is supported by statistics that demonstrate that an increasing number of innocent defendants are being found on death row. Unfortunately, most prisoners under sentence of death are not lucky or wealthy enough to receive the kind of dedicated legal representation necessary to put on an adequate defense. Expert testimony is costly, and not readily available to the indigent defendant.

According to the Death Penalty Information Center (DPIC), since 1973, 127 people in 26 states have been released from death row with evidence of their innocence. These defendants appear on the DPIC's "Innocence List."

In order to be included on the list, the defendant must have been convicted, sentenced to death and subsequently either (1) their conviction was overturned, and they were either (a) acquitted at trial; or (b) all charges were dropped; or (2) they were given an absolute pardon by the governor based on new evidence of innocence.

Tables setting forth a list of death row prisoners exonerated by state and by year may be found in Appendices 13 and 14, respectively, of this Almanac.

Recent Death Row Exoneration Cases

Levon Jones

The most recent release from death row occurred on May 2, 2008. Levon Jones was convicted of murder and sentenced to death in North Carolina in 1993. He spent 13 years on death row. The presiding judge criticized the defense attorneys for "constitutionally deficient" performance, noting their failure to research the history and credibility of the prosecution's star witness. A sworn affidavit submitted by Jones' new defense team in which the key witness stated that her testimony was untrue, that a detective coached her testimony, and that she received $4,000 in return for information that led to Jones' arrest. These facts supported Jones' innocence and led to his release and exoneration.

Glen Edward Chapman

Glen Edward Chapman was released from death row on April 2, 2008. Chapman was convicted of a double murder and sentenced to death in North Carolina in 1994. He spent 14 years on death row. The presiding judge cited withheld evidence, lost, misplaced or destroyed documents, the use of weak and circumstantial evidence, false testimony by the lead investigator, and ineffective assistance of defense counsel, as reasons for the release. One of the defense lawyers had been disciplined by the North Carolina State Bar, and the other defense attorney admitted to drinking 12 shots of alcohol per day during a different death penalty trial that resulted in the execution of the defendant in 2001. In addition, there was new information from a forensic pathologist that raised doubts as to whether one of the deaths was a homicide or a drug overdose. These facts led to Chapman's release.

Kennedy Brewer

Kennedy Brewer was released from death row on February 8, 2008. Brewer was convicted of murder and sentenced to death in Mississippi in 1995. He spent 12 years on death row. Post-conviction DNA testing on evidence from the crime scene in Brewer's case implicated another man in the crime. The DNA profile matched a local man, who later confessed to killing the child. The DNA testing, combined with the confession, demonstrated Brewer's innocence and led to his release and exoneration. Brewer was released on bail in 2007, and his charges were dismissed in 2008.

This case raised dozens of serious questions about the way forensic science is performed in Mississippi. The medical examiner was not properly board-certified and did not comply with basic professional standards. The expert had been expelled from professional associations and discredited.

Curtis McCarty

Curtis Edward McCarty was exonerated in 2007 after serving 21 years, including nearly 18 years on death row, for a 1982 Oklahoma City murder he didn't commit. McCarty was convicted twice and sentenced to death three times based on prosecutorial misconduct and testimony from the forensic analyst, whose lab misconduct has contributed to at least two other convictions later overturned by DNA evidence.

Ryan Matthews

Ryan Matthews was exonerated in 2004 after serving 5 years on Louisiana's death row for a crime he did not commit. Matthews was 17 years old at the time he was arrested. He was subsequently sentenced to death for the shooting death of a convenience store owner based on eyewitness misidentification. DNA testing results both exonerated Matthews and revealed the identity of the actual perpetrator.

Nicholas Yarris

Nicholas Yarris was exonerated in 2003 after serving 21-1/2 years on death row in Pennsylvania. In 1982, Yarris was convicted of murder, rape, and abduction, and sentenced to death, based on eyewitness misidentification, unreliable and limited science, and unreliable jailhouse informant testimony. In 1989, he became one of Pennsylvania's first death row inmates to demand post-conviction DNA testing to prove his innocence. Based on the testing results, the court vacated Yarris' conviction and he became the 140th person in the United States to be exonerated by post-conviction DNA testing, and the 13th DNA exoneration from death row.

Ray Krone

Ray Krone was exonerated in 2002 after serving 10 years on Arizona's death row. In 1992, Krone was found guilty of murder and kidnapping, and sentenced to death based on unreliable and limited scientific evidence and forensic misconduct. It was not until 2002, that DNA testing conducted on the saliva and blood found on the victim excluded Krone as the source and instead matched another man.

Charles Irvin Fain

Charles Irvin Fain was exonerated in 2001 after serving 17-1/2 years on Idaho's death row. Fain was convicted and sentenced to death for the murder, rape, and kidnapping of a young girl based on unreliable and limited scientific evidence and unreliable informant testimony Mitochondrial DNA testing revealed that the hairs used as evidence at trial did not belong to Fain. Based on this new evidence, a judge ordered his release. Fain became the eleventh person in the United States to be freed from death row due to post-conviction DNA testing.

Frank Lee Smith

Frank Lee Smith was exonerated in 2000 after serving 14 years on Florida's death row. Smith was convicted of the rape and murder of an 8-year old child based on eyewitness misidentification. Unfortunately, Smith died of cancer on January 30, 2000, before he was exonerated of rape and murder. On December 15, 2000, eleven months after his death, Smith was exonerated based on exculpatory DNA testing results. These results not only cleared Smith of the crime, but identified the true perpetrator.

Earl Washington

Earl Washington was exonerated in 2000 after serving 17 years on Virginia's death row. Washington was a twenty-two year old black man with a general I.Q. in the range of 69 when he was arrested for rape and murder. He was subsequently convicted and sentenced to death based on his false confessions and admissions. In October 1993, DNA testing results excluded Washington as the perpetrator, however, the evidence was time-barred under Virginia law. On January 14, 1994, Governor Wilder commuted Washington's sentence to life imprisonment. Washington remained in prison for six more years before his attorney was able to persuade the newly elected Governor Gilmore to obtain additional DNA testing. On October 2, 2000, Governor Gilmore announced the results of the DNA test and granted Washington an absolute pardon for the capital murder conviction.

Execution of Innocent Defendants

It is impossible to determine how many innocent people have been executed since the death penalty was reinstated in 1976. However, according to the National Coalition to Abolish the Death Penalty and the Death Penalty Information Center, in the following cases, there was strong evidence that the executed prisoner was innocent:

Ruben Cantu

Ruben Cantu was convicted of murder in 1985 at the age of 17, and executed in Texas in 1993. Cantu had persistently proclaimed his innocence. The prosecutor and the jury forewoman have since expressed serious doubts about the case. In addition, a key eyewitness against Cantu recanted his testimony, and Cantu's co-defendant has stated that Cantu was innocent of the crime.

Carlos DeLuna

Carlos DeLuna was convicted of murder in 1983 and executed in Texas in 1989. New evidence uncovered in 2006 cast serious doubt on DeLuna's guilt, insofar as another man, who had a record of similar crimes, repeatedly confessed to the murder.

Gary Graham

Gary Graham was convicted of murder in 1981 and executed in Texas in 2000, despite claims he was innocent. Graham was 17 at the time of the murder, and was convicted primarily on the unreliable testimony of one witness. Two other witnesses who claimed Graham was not the killer were never interviewed by Graham's attorney and were not called to testify at trial.

Larry Griffin

Larry Griffin was convicted of murder in 1981 and executed in Missouri in 1995. Griffin maintained his innocence until his death, and new eyewitness evidence demonstrates that he was not involved in the crime for which he was convicted.

Leonel Herrera

Leonel Herrera was executed in Texas in 1993 despite compelling evidence of his innocence. A former Texas judge submitted an affidavit stating that another man had confessed to the crime for which Herrera was facing execution. Numerous other pieces of new evidence also threw doubt on his conviction. According to the Supreme Court, however, that proof was not sufficient to stop his execution because of the late stage of his appeal.

Jesse Jacobs

Jesse Jacobs was executed in Texas in 1995 despite the prosecution's admission that arguments they made at Jacobs' trial were false. Jacobs was convicted after the state introduced evidence that Jacobs, rather than his co-defendant, pulled the trigger on the day of the murder. At the subsequent trial of the co-defendant, the state reversed its story and said it was the co-defendant, not Jacobs, who pulled the trigger. The prosecution later vouched for the credibility of Jacobs' testimony that he did not commit the shooting and did not even know that his co-defendant had a gun. Jacobs' co-defendant was also convicted, though he was not sentenced to death.

Leo Jones

Leo Jones was convicted of murdering a police officer in 1981 and executed in Florida in 1998. Jones claimed that his confession was coerced following several hours of police interrogation, one of whom was identified by a fellow officer as an "enforcer" who used torture. In addition, many witnesses came forward pointing to another suspect in the case.

Robert Nelson

Robert Nelson was executed in Texas in 1994 after being denied a new hearing even though another man signed a sworn affidavit confessing to the murder, thus exonerating Drew.

Joseph O'Dell

Joseph O'Dell was convicted of murder in 1986 and executed in Virginia in 1997 despite the existence of DNA blood evidence that could have proved his innocence. The courts refused to consider the new evidence because, under Virginia law, any evidence found after 21 days could not be used to prove the innocence of a convicted person.

David Spence

David Spence was convicted of murder in 1984 and executed in Texas in 1997 despite the lack of evidence connecting him to the crime, and the reliance on testimony of prison inmates who were granted favors in return for the testimony that helped convict Spence.

Cameron Willingham

Cameron Willingham was convicted of arson-related murder in 1992 and executed in Texas in 2004. Willingham consistently proclaimed his innocence. After examining evidence from the case, four national arson experts concluded that the original investigation of Willingham's case was flawed and it is possible the fire, which killed Willingham's three children, was accidental.

COMPENSATION FOR WRONGFUL INCARCERATION

When an innocent person is wrongfully convicted of a crime and incarcerated, they face numerous difficulties trying to readjust to society. They have lost their freedom, often for many, many years, during which time they were subjected to the nightmare of the prison experience, not knowing whether they would ever be exonerated.

During their imprisonment, many convicts are abandoned by their family, and lose custody of their children. Once they are released, without an extensive support system, and without any funds, they must find employment, housing, and health care, and a way to reconnect with the outside world. It is only fair, that the states which wrongfully convicted them in the first place, assist them in this transition. Legal services, health services, housing, job counseling and placement, and financial assistance are necessary components of a successful transition.

The federal government, 22 states and the District of Columbia have enacted some type of law compensating those who have been wrongfully incarcerated, including: Alabama, California, Illinois, Iowa, Louisiana, Maine, Maryland, Massachusetts, Missouri, Montana, New Hampshire, New Jersey, New York, North Carolina, Ohio, Oklahoma, Tennessee, Texas, Vermont, Virginia, West Virginia, and Wisconsin. Compensation varies depending on the state.

MODEL PENAL CODE RECOMMENDATIONS

Following the 1972 *Furman* decision, when the United States Supreme Court overturned existing death penalty statutes, many states re-wrote their laws according to the recommendations set forth in the American Law Institute (ALI) Model Penal Code.

In the 1976 *Gregg* decision, when the Supreme Court began to approve of the newly rewritten death penalty statutes, the Court specifically referred to the Model Penal Code as a source for constructing a constitutionally acceptable statute.

The drafters of the Model Penal Code were aware of the danger that an innocent person could be convicted and sentenced to death by a jury despite the existence of "reasonable doubt." They addressed this concern by inserting a provision that permits the trial court to withhold a death sentence if there was evidence that left some doubt about the defendant's guilt, as follows:

> **Section 210.6 Sentence of Death for Murder; Further Proceedings to Determine Sentence.**
>
> (1) Death Sentence Excluded. When a defendant is found guilty of murder, the Court shall impose sentence for a felony of the first degree (i.e., a non-death sentence) if it is satisfied that: . . . (f) although the evidence suffices to sustain the verdict, it does not foreclose all doubt respecting the defendant's guilt.

In its commentary, the ALI set forth its reasoning for inserting this provision:

> [S]usbsection (1)(f) . . . is an accommodation to the irrevocability of the capital sanction. Where doubt of guilt remains, the opportunity to reverse a conviction on the basis of new evidence must be preserved, and a sentence of death is obviously inconsistent with that goal.

Nevertheless, no state or federal jurisdiction adopted this provision, instead opting to include only a list of aggravating and mitigating circumstances for capital cases as also suggested by the Model Penal Code.

CHAPTER 6:
DEMOGRAPHICS

RACE AND THE DEATH PENALTY

In *Furman v. Georgia*, 408 U.S. 238 (1972), the U.S. Supreme Court ruled that the death penalty was unconstitutional, and pointed out that racial discrimination was one of the grounds for its decision. Among other things, the Court held that the unlimited discretion allowed judges and juries in capital cases caused the death penalty to be applied in an "arbitrary and capricious" manner.

Four years later, in *Gregg v. Georgia*, 428 U.S. 153 (1976) the Supreme Court reinstated the death penalty, and held that the rewritten statutes provided adequate safeguards against arbitrariness and discrimination.

Nevertheless, subsequent evidence demonstrates that racial bias has continued to influence death sentencing. It is a fact that a disproportionate number of black prisoners have faced execution on death row compared to their percentage of the total population. Between 1930 and 1996, 4,220 prisoners were executed in the United States; and more than half of those executed were black.

Throughout the 20th century, black defendants were routinely executed for offenses that would not have been considered a capital offense for a white defendant, such as rape. In fact, between 1930 and 1976, 455 men were executed for rape, and 405 of those executed were black.

In addition, a greater number of black juveniles were executed than white, and the rate of execution for blacks who did not have any post-conviction appeal is also higher.

Although it is believed that this type of blatant racial bias no longer exists, present statistics demonstrate that blacks still make up a disproportionately large percentage of death row prisoners. For example, of the 3,228 prisoners on death row in 2006, 41% were black.

A table setting forth the number of prisoners under sentence of death categorized by race from 1968 through 2006 may be found in Appendix 15 of this Almanac.

Statistics

Since the death penalty was reinstated in 1976, 1,099 convicted prisoners have been executed in the United States as of Oct 1, 2007. Of those executed, 625 (57%) were white, 374 (34%) were black, and 24 (2%) were categorized as "other."

Between 1977 and 2006, 7,433 prisoners were on death row. Of this total, 3,633 (48.8%) were white, 3,047 (41%) were black, 636 (8.6%) were Hispanic, and 117 (1.6%) were categorized as "other."

As of January 2007, there were 3,350 prisoners under sentence of death. Of this total, 1,517 (45.3%) were white, 1,397 (41.7%) were black, 359 (10.7%) were Hispanic, and 77 (2.3%) were classified as "other."

Between 1976 and July 2007, there were a total of 1,087 prisoners executed. Of those executed, there were 621 whites (57%), 367 blacks (34%), 75 Hispanics (7%), 15 Native Americans (1%), and 9 prisoners categorized as "other," which includes Asian Pacific Islanders and those categorized as "unknowns" (1%).

Since 1973, there have been 127 people released from death row with evidence of innocence. Of that total, 64 (50%) prisoners were black, 50 (39%) prisoners were white, 12 (9%) prisoners were Hispanic, and 1 prisoner was classified as "other."

The Race of the Victim

Although blacks continue to be sentenced to death and executed in far greater numbers than their proportion to the total population, many studies concerning this racial disparity suggest that the race of the victim is the decisive factor. Based on a number of studies, in 1990 the United States General Accounting Office concluded that prisoners on death row are more likely to have been convicted of a crime in which the victim was white.

According to a comprehensive study of racial discrimination and the death penalty in the state of Georgia, the odds of being sentenced to death were 4.3 times higher in cases where the victims were white. Thus, it is still a fact that the killing of a white person is treated much more severely than the killing of a black person. This is so regardless of the race of the offender.

U.S. Supreme Court Justice Harry Blackmun, who was always a supporter of the death penalty even when it was outlawed in 1972, concluded that racial discrimination continues to corrupt the administration of capital punishment, stating: "Even under the most sophisticated death penalty statutes, race continues to play a major role in determining who shall live and who shall die."

WOMEN AND THE DEATH PENALTY

Over the past twenty years, a very small percentage of women have been sentenced to death, and an even smaller number of women on death row have actually been executed. Statistics show that women are more likely to be dropped out of the system as they advance further through the phases of capital punishment case administration.

Statistics

Since the death penalty was reinstated in 1976, 1,099 convicted murderers have been executed in the United States as of Oct 1, 2007. Of those executed, 11 were female. The last woman executed was Frances Elaine Newton in Texas on September 14, 2005.

The rate of death sentencing of women is insignificant compared to men. Women account for about 1 in 8 murder arrests, which is approximately 13% of the total. Nevertheless, women account for only 1 in 50 death sentences imposed at the trial level. As of December 31, 2006, of the 3,228 prisoners under sentence of death, only 54 (1.7%) were women.

A table of the number of women prisoners under sentence of death as of December 31, 2006, categorized by state and race may be found in Appendix 16 of this Almanac.

Executions

Eleven women have been executed since the resumption of executions in 1977. The first was Velma Barfield, who was put to death in North Carolina by lethal injection on November 2, 1984.

Another case involved Judy Buenoano, a 54-year old white woman who was convicted of, among other things, poisoning her husbands with arsenic. Ms. Buenoano—known as the "Black Widow"—was executed in Florida by electrocution on March 30, 1998. She was the first woman to be executed in Florida since 1838.

A month prior, on February 3, 1998, another white woman named Karla Faye Tucker was executed in Texas, after exhausting all of her appeals. Unlike Ms. Buenoano, there was a massive public movement to spare

Ms. Tucker's life due to her apparently sincere conversion since her conviction for the brutal murder of two people with an axe. Nevertheless, her last minute petition for clemency was denied by Governor George Bush, and she was executed by lethal injection.

Betty Lou Beets was executed by injection in Texas on February 24, 2000 for murdering her husband.

Christina Marie Riggs also received a lethal injection for the murder of her two small children on May 3, 2000 in Arkansas. She fought strenuously for the right to die.

During 2001, Oklahoma emptied its female death row by executing all three women on it. Wanda Jean Allen became the first black woman to be executed since 1954, and the first in Oklahoma since 1903, when she was given a lethal injection on January 11, 2001 for the murder of her lesbian lover.

The execution of Marilyn Kay Plantz followed on May 1, 2001, for organizing the murder of her husband. One of her male accomplices was also executed for his part in the killing.

Lois Nadean Smith was executed for the July 4, 1982 murder of 21-year old Cindy Baillee, whom she suspected of plotting to murder her son, Greg. She was given a lethal injection at the Oklahoma State Penitentiary on December 4, 2001.

On May 10, 2002, Lynda Lyon Block became what most believe will be the last woman to suffer death in the electric chair when she was executed in Alabama for the murder of a police officer on October 4, 1993.

Serial killer, Aileen Wournos, was put to death by lethal injection in Florida on October 9, 2002 for the robbery/murder of Richard Mallory. She confessed to killing 6 other men and her execution was consensual.

There were no female executions in 2003 and 2004 and four women were taken off death row in Illinois when Governor Ryan decided to commute all death sentences in that state.

Finally, Frances Elaine Newton was executed by lethal injection in Texas on September 14, 2005, having been convicted of killing her husband and two children to gain $100,000 in insurance benefits in 1987.

AGE AND THE DEATH PENALTY

Juvenile Offenders

When the death penalty was reinstated in 1976, over sixteen states permitted the execution of offenders who were younger than 18 years of age. In 14 states, the death penalty could not be imposed unless the offender was 18 or older. The federal government also specified age 18 as the minimum age for a death penalty sentence. Eight states did not specify any minimum age.

The trend towards abolishing the death penalty for juvenile offenders began in 1988 with the abolition of capital punishment for offenders under the age of 16. After initially upholding the death penalty for juvenile offenders aged 16 and 17, the United States Supreme Court finally abolished capital punishment for all juvenile offenders in 2005.

Thompson v. Oklahoma

In 1988, the United States Supreme Court abolished capital punishment for offenders under the age of 16 in *Thompson v. Oklahoma*, 487 U.S. 815 (1988).

William W. Thompson, who was 15 at the time of his crime, was tried as an adult for murder, found guilty, and sentenced to death in an Oklahoma trial court. The Court of Criminal Appeals of Oklahoma upheld the decision.

Thompson appealed the decision to the U.S. Supreme Court. In a 5-4 decision, the Court held that Thompson's execution would violate the Eighth Amendment prohibition against cruel and unusual punishment. The Court noted the "evolving standards of decency that mark the progress of a maturing society" as a primary concern. Numerous U.S. jurisdictions and all industrialized Western nations had banned the execution of minors under 16 years of age.

Stanford v. Kentucky

In 1989, the United States Supreme Court upheld the possibility of capital punishment for offenders who were 16 or 17 years old when they committed the capital offense in *Stanford v. Kentucky*, 492 U.S. 361 (1989).

Kevin Stanford, who was 17 at the time of his crime, was tried as an adult for sodomy and murder, found guilty, and sentenced to death in a Kentucky trial court. The Kentucky Supreme Court upheld the decision.

Stanford appealed the decision to the U.S. Supreme Court. In a 5-4 decision, the Court held that Stanford's punishment did not "offend the Eighth Amendment's prohibition against cruel and unusual punishment," and affirmed the lower court's decision.

In 2003, however, the Governor of Kentucky commuted the death sentence of Kevin Stanford.

Roper v. Simmons

In 2005, the United States Supreme Court abolished capital punishment for all juveniles in *Roper v. Simmons*, 543 U.S. 551 (2005).

Christopher Simmons, who was 17 at the time of his crime, was tried as an adult for murder, found guilty, and sentenced to death in a Missouri trial court. On appeal, the Missouri Supreme Court reversed the lower court and sentenced Simmons to life imprisonment without parole.

The State of Missouri appealed the decision to the U.S. Supreme Court. In a 5-4 decision, the Court held that it is unconstitutional to impose capital punishment for crimes committed while under the age of 18.

Under the "evolving standards of decency" test, the Court held that it was cruel and unusual punishment to execute a person who was under the age of 18 at the time of the murder. Writing for the majority, Justice Kennedy cited a body of sociological and scientific research that found that juveniles have a lack of maturity and sense of responsibility compared to adults. Adolescents were found to be overrepresented statistically in virtually every category of reckless behavior.

The Court also noted that in recognition of the comparative immaturity and irresponsibility of juveniles, almost every state prohibited those under age 18 from voting, serving on juries, or marrying without parental consent. The studies also found that juveniles are also more vulnerable to negative influences and outside pressures, including peer pressure.

In support of the "national consensus" position, the Court noted the increasing infrequency with which states were applying capital punishment for juvenile offenders, and also cited international law to support the holding.

The Court noted that, since 1990, only seven other countries, including Iran, Pakistan, Saudi Arabia, Yemen, Nigeria, the Democratic Republic of Congo, and China, had executed defendants who were juveniles at the time of their crime, and that each of those countries had either abolished the death penalty for juveniles or publicly disavowed the practice. Thus, the United States stood alone in allowing execution of juvenile offenders.

EXECUTION OF THE ELDERLY

The death row population is aging, and prison conditions are not conducive to good health. Thus, there has been much controversy recently over the constitutionality of executing the elderly and infirm. The execution of a lame, deaf and infirm senior, regardless of the crime that placed them on death row, is a task that few prison wardens are comfortable with carrying out.

Nevertheless, the United States Supreme Court has thus far refused to ban capital punishment for the elderly on the basis that the punishment is cruel and unusual.

Statistics

According to the U.S. Bureau of Justice Statistics, as of December 31, 2006, a record 153 prisoners aged 60 and older were on death rows across the nation. In California alone, there are presently four condemned men who are over 70, and nearly three dozen in their 60s. Since California reinstated capital punishment, 31 men have died on death row of natural causes.

Causes

Death row's elderly population has grown for several reasons. A few seniors are on death row because they committed a capital offense at an unusually old age. However, most are there because death penalty appeals can go on for decades. For example, one North Carolina convict began appealing his murder conviction in 1966, when he was 27. It has been set aside and reinstated twice, and he is now in his late 60s.

A table of the number of prisoners under sentence of death as of December 31, 2006 categorized by age, may be found in Appendix 17 of this Almanac.

Clarence Ray Allen

Clarence Ray Allen was a convicted murderer when he was sentenced to death in 1982 for paying a fellow inmate to kill three witnesses in his murder case. On January 17, 2006, despite being legally blind, nearly deaf, diabetic, and confined to a wheelchair, 76-year old Allen was executed by lethal injection by the State of California.

Allen appealed to Governor Arnold Schwarzenegger for clemency on grounds of his age, serious illnesses, and the alleged unfairness of his 1982 trial. Governor Schwarzenegger rejected Allen's appeal for clemency.

Allen's attorneys then made a last minute appeal to the U.S. Supreme Court to stop the execution citing his age and ill health. They argued that the death penalty was cruel and unusual punishment for someone so old and frail. However, the Court rejected the last minute appeal.

Allen was California's oldest death row inmate to be executed, and the second oldest in the United States since the ban on capital punishment was lifted in 1976.

John B. Nixon, Sr.

Despite the execution of Clarence Ray Allen, California cannot claim the U.S. record for killing the oldest person since the death penalty was reinstated. That record is held by Mississippi for the execution of 77-year old John B. Nixon, Sr. on December 14, 2005.

Nixon had been on death row for 20 years. He was convicted in 1985 for the slaying of Virginia Tucker. Three other persons, including Nixon's sons, John B. Nixon, Jr. and Henry L. Nixon, were also convicted in connection with the murder. They were allegedly paid to do the killing by Tucker's former husband. Nixon maintained his innocence and said, just before his execution, that another of his sons committed the murder.

CHAPTER 7:
MENTAL DISABILITIES AND THE DEATH PENALTY

IN GENERAL

The execution of mentally disabled individuals has long been a controversial topic. Generally, mentally disabled individuals are categorized as either mentally retarded or mentally ill, and their rights differ depending on the diagnosis.

MENTAL RETARDATION

Mental Retardation Defined

Mental retardation is defined differently from mental illness. According to the American Heritage Dictionary, mental retardation is indicated by subnormal intellectual development as a result of congenital causes, brain injury, or disease and characterized by any of various cognitive deficiencies, including impaired learning, social, and vocational ability.

The Ban on Execution of the Mentally Retarded

The execution of the mentally retarded is no longer permitted in the United States. On June 20, 2002, in a 6-3 decision, the Supreme Court issued a landmark ruling holding that the execution of those with mental retardation is unconstitutional (*Atkins v. Virginia*, 536 U.S. 304 (2002)).

Atkins v. Virginia

Petitioner Atkins was convicted of capital murder and related crimes by a Virginia jury, and sentenced to death. On appeal, the Virginia Supreme Court affirmed the conviction and rejected petitioner's contention that he could not be sentenced to death because he is mentally retarded.

The U.S. Supreme Court reversed the Virginia Supreme Court, and held that it is a violation of the Eighth Amendment ban on cruel and unusual punishment to execute death row inmates with mental retardation.

In its ruling, the Court opined that a punishment is "excessive," and therefore prohibited by the Eighth Amendment, if it is not graduated and proportioned to the offense. The Court noted that an excessiveness claim is judged by currently prevailing standards of decency. The Court cited the fact that a significant number of states have concluded that death is not a suitable punishment for a mentally retarded criminal, and similar bills have passed at least one house in other states. The Court further stated that the states' actions provide powerful evidence that present-day society views mentally retarded offenders as categorically less culpable than the average criminal.

The Court also found that, although mentally retarded persons frequently know the difference between right and wrong, and are competent to stand trial, they have diminished capacities to understand and process information, to communicate, to abstract from mistakes and learn from experience, to engage in logical reasoning, to control impulses, and to understand others' reactions. The Court further stated that, although deficiencies do not warrant an exemption from criminal sanctions, they do diminish one's personal culpability.

The Court set forth its reasoning for its ruling by addressing the factors that purportedly justify capital punishment—retribution and deterrence—as well as the danger of wrongful execution.

Retribution

The Court found that the severity of the appropriate punishment necessarily depends on the offender's culpability. Thus, if the culpability of the average murderer is insufficient to justify imposition of death, the lesser culpability of the mentally retarded offender surely does not merit that form of retribution.

Deterrence

The Court found that the same cognitive and behavioral impairments that make mentally retarded defendants less morally culpable also make it less likely that they can process the information of the possibility of execution as a penalty and, as a result, control their conduct based upon that information.

Further, the Court stated that exempting the mentally retarded from execution will not lessen the death penalty's deterrent effect with respect to offenders who are not mentally retarded.

Wrongful Execution

The Court found that mentally retarded defendants in the aggregate face a special risk of wrongful execution because of the possibility that they will unwittingly confess to crimes they did not commit, their lesser ability to give their counsel meaningful assistance, and the facts that they are typically poor witnesses and that their demeanor may create an unwarranted impression of lack of remorse for their crimes.

The IQ Factor

In 2007, the California Supreme Court unanimously ruled that a defendant may be spared the death penalty because he is mentally deficient in one area, even if his IQ score falls in the normal range. The court ruled that trial courts may give greater weight to certain kinds of evidence than others because the legal definition of mental retardation does not rely on a fixed IQ score.

The Court rejected a lower court holding that "full scale" IQ scores are the best way to measure intellectual functioning. The Justices ruled that the best way to measure intellectual functioning may vary from case to case, and the law should not dictate how to measure intellectual functioning.

A table of state statutes defining mental retardation for the purpose of the imposition of the death penalty may be found in Appendix 18 of this Almanac.

A list of defendants with mental retardation executed in the United States since reinstatement of the death penalty in 1976 may be found in Appendix 19 of this Almanac.

MENTAL ILLNESS

Mental Illness Defined

Unlike mental retardation, which is a permanent developmental disability, mental illness is not necessarily present all of the time in an individual, due to either treatment or remission. According to the American Heritage Dictionary, mental illness is defined as any of various conditions characterized by impairment of an individual's normal cognitive, emotional, or behavioral functioning, and caused by social, psychological, biochemical, genetic, or other factors, such as infection or head trauma.

Mental illness is also referred to as emotional illness, mental disease, and mental disorder, and can incorporate a wide range of conditions, some more serious than others.

Mental Disorders

The National Association of Mental Health has estimated that 5–10% of the U.S. death row population has serious mental illness. Some of the more common mental illnesses experienced by inmates on death row, as defined by the National Institute of Mental Health, may include the following:

Bipolar Disorder

Bipolar Disorder, also known as manic-depressive illness, is a serious medical illness that causes shifts in a person's mood, energy, and ability to function. These mood shifts are different from the normal ups and downs that many people experience.

The symptoms of bipolar disorder are severe. Bipolar disorder causes dramatic mood swings from overly "high" and/or irritable to sad and hopeless, and then back again, often with periods of normal mood in between. Severe changes in energy and behavior go along with these changes in mood. The periods of highs and lows are called episodes of mania and depression.

Most people with bipolar disorder can achieve substantial stabilization of their mood swings and related symptoms over time with proper treatment that combines medication and psychosocial treatment.

Borderline Personality Disorder

Borderline personality disorder (BPD) is a serious mental illness characterized by pervasive instability in moods, interpersonal relationships, self-image, and behavior. This instability often disrupts family and work life, long-term planning, and the individual's sense of self-identity. While less well known than schizophrenia or bipolar disorder, BPD is more common, affecting 2% of adults.

While a person with depression or bipolar disorder typically endures the same mood for weeks, a person with BPD may experience intense bouts of anger, depression, and anxiety that may last only hours, or at most a day. These episodes may be associated with impulsive aggression, self-injury, and drug or alcohol abuse. Sometimes people with BPD view themselves as fundamentally bad, or unworthy. They may feel unfairly misunderstood or mistreated, bored, empty, and have little idea who they are. Such symptoms are most acute when people with BPD feel isolated and lacking in social support, and may result in frantic efforts to avoid being alone.

People with BPD often have highly unstable patterns of social relationships. While they can develop intense but stormy attachments, their attitudes towards family, friends, and loved ones may suddenly shift from idealization, i.e., great admiration and love, to devaluation, i.e., intense anger and dislike. BPD often occurs together with other psychiatric problems, particularly bipolar disorder, depression, anxiety disorders, substance abuse, and other personality disorders.

There is a high rate of self-injury without suicide intent, as well as a significant rate of suicide attempts and completed suicide in severe cases. Patients often need extensive mental health services, and account for 20% of psychiatric hospitalizations.

Treatments for BPD include group and individual psychotherapy. Within the past 15 years, a new psychosocial treatment termed dialectical behavior therapy (DBT) was developed specifically to treat BPD. In addition, pharmacological treatments are often prescribed based on specific target symptoms shown by the individual patient, e.g., antidepressant drugs and mood stabilizers may be helpful for depression, and antipsychotic drugs may be used when there are distortions in thinking.

Brain Damage

Serious brain damage may be equivalent to mental retardation, but is not defined as mental retardation because it occurred not as a lifelong developmental disability, but as the result of an accident or other traumatic event.

Organic brain syndrome is a general term referring to physical disorders of the brain arising from disease or trauma that cause decreased mental function such as problems with attention, concentration and memory, confusion, anxiety and depression.

Depression

Major depression is a serious medical illness affecting nearly 10 million people in America in any given year. It can significantly interfere with an individual's thoughts, behavior, mood, activity, and physical health. Left untreated, depression can lead to suicide. It is more than just feeling "down in the dumps" or "blue" for a few days. It is feeling "down" and "low" and "hopeless" for weeks at a time.

The signs and symptoms of depression include persistent sad, anxious, or "empty" mood; feelings of hopelessness and pessimism; feelings of guilt, worthlessness, and helplessness; and loss of interest or pleasure in hobbies and activities that were once enjoyed. There are a variety of treatments for depression including medications and short-term psychotherapies.

Dissociative Disorder

Dissociative disorder is characterized by a dissociation from a person's fundamental aspects of consciousness, such as one's identity and history. There are many forms of dissociative disorder, the best known of which is dissociative identity disorder—formerly known as multiple personality disorder—where an individual has one or more distinct identities or personalities that surface on a recurring basis. All of the dissociative disorders are thought to stem from trauma experienced by the sufferer.

Post-Traumatic Stress Disorder

Post-Traumatic Stress Disorder (PTSD) is an anxiety disorder that can develop after exposure to a terrifying event or ordeal in which grave physical harm occurred or was threatened. Traumatic events that may trigger PTSD include violent personal assaults, natural or human-caused disasters, accidents, or military combat.

People with PTSD have persistent frightening thoughts and memories of their ordeal and feel emotionally numb, especially with people they were once close to. They may experience sleep problems, outbursts of anger, feelings of detachment or numbness, or be easily startled. Effective treatments for post-traumatic stress disorder are available.

Schizophrenia

Schizophrenia is a chronic, severe, and disabling brain disorder that affects about 1.1% of the U.S. population age 18 and older in a given year. The World Health Organization (WHO) has identified schizophrenia as one of the 10 most debilitating diseases affecting humans.

People with schizophrenia sometimes hear voices others don't hear, believe that others are broadcasting their thoughts to the world, or become convinced that others are plotting to harm them. These experiences can make sufferers fearful and withdrawn and cause difficulties when they try to have relationships with others.

Symptoms of schizophrenia can include hallucinations, delusions, disordered thinking, movement disorders, flat affect, social withdrawal, and cognitive deficits. Although the causes of the disease have not yet been determined, current treatments can eliminate many of the symptoms.

Extending the Atkins Ruling to the Mentally Ill

As set forth above, in June 2002, the U.S. Supreme Court determined in the case of *Atkins v. Virginia* that executing a mentally retarded individual amounted to "cruel and unusual punishment." The court reasoned that a mentally retarded defendant had diminished personal culpability in the crime.

Medical and legal scholars argue that the same reasoning should apply to mentally ill defendants. The National Alliance on Mental Illness believes that "persons who have committed offenses due to states of mind or behavior caused by a brain disorder require treatment, not punishment." Thus, it is argued that it is arbitrary to exempt people with mental retardation from execution while those with serious mental illness at the time of the crime are able to be executed.

In addition, according to a dissenting opinion by an Indiana Supreme Court justice, "the underlying rationale for prohibiting executions of the mentally retarded is just as compelling for prohibiting executions of the seriously mentally ill, namely evolving standards of decency."

The problem is, however, that mental health experts and legal scholars have not been able to agree what the term "mental illness" should mean when seeking to extend the *Atkins* protection to people with mental illness. Thus, people with serious mental illness continue to be sentenced to death and executed in the United States.

According to the American Psychiatric Association, from a biopsychosocial perspective, primary mental retardation and significant mental disorders have similar etiological characteristics. Thus, the mentally ill suffer from many of the same limitations that "do not warrant an exemption from criminal sanctions, but they do diminish their personal culpability," as set forth in the *Atkins* decision.

Further, in *Atkins*, a part of the reason for prohibiting the execution of offenders with mental retardation was that "in the aggregate, they face a special risk of wrongful execution." By this, the Court not only meant that the particular vulnerabilities of such individuals placed them at a higher risk of wrongful conviction, but also placed them at an increased risk of being sentenced to death whereas a non-impaired individual might receive a life prison term.

According to Amnesty International, a death penalty abolitionist organization, a mentally ill defendant who has committed a capital offense may be at heightened and unfair risk of receiving a death sentence compared to defendants with no or lesser impairments, or in some cases being wrongfully convicted, for the following reasons:

1. Even if found competent to stand trial, the defendant's capacity to assist their lawyer or understand the proceedings may still be impaired;

2. As a part of their illness, a defendant suffering from a mental condition such as severe depression or a paranoid disorder may refuse to allow mitigation to be presented or may even plead guilty and demand the death sentence.

3. Due to the stigma attached to mental illness, particularly if it is linked to a family history of such illness or to childhood abuse, a defendant may seek to downplay his or her ailment or simply not report it to defense counsel.

4. If the defendant's mental illness is still showing symptoms at the time of the trial, he or she may act irrationally or appear to do so to jurors, heightening fears of future dangerousness, a highly aggravating factor in the minds of capital jurors.

5. A mentally ill defendant, especially if taking medication at the time of the trial, may display a flat affect and be perceived as remorseless, another highly aggravating factor in the mind of capital jurors.

6. A mentally ill defendant may be particularly difficult to represent for an under-resourced or inexperienced defense lawyer.

7. A mentally ill defendant may be particularly vulnerable to unscrupulous prosecutors or police.

8. Jurors ignorant of or frightened by mental illness, or suspicious of the state's capacity to appropriately treat the mentally ill, may be swayed towards a death sentence, fearing the defendant's propensity for future violence.

9. If the defendant's crime was committed as a result of mental illness, it may appear motiveless. Thus, the offence may display a senseless brutality, further heightening the jury's fears about future dangerousness.

Recent Executions Involving the Mentally Ill

Troy Kunkle (Schizophrenia)

At the time of the crime, Troy Kunkle was just over 18 years old, with no criminal record, and emerging from a childhood of deprivation and abuse. His parents had been diagnosed with mental illness.

In post-conviction evaluations, a psychologist concluded that Troy Kunkle was suffering from schizophrenia, a diagnosis he said was backed up by prison records. The psychologist concluded that an expert evaluation at the time of the trial would likely have shown Troy Kunkle's emerging mental disorder. The jury heard no expert testimony.

Troy Kunkle was executed in Texas in 2005.

Donald Beardslee (Severe Brain Damage)

Donald Beardslee's clemency lawyers revealed evidence of his mental impairment. An expert conducted an assessment of Beardslee and concluded that he suffered from severe brain damage, and that the right hemisphere of his brain was virtually non-functioning. The expert concluded that in all likelihood he had suffered from this impairment since birth and it was exacerbated by serious head injuries he sustained when a teenager and in his early 20s. The expert also concluded that the brain damage likely affected his behavior at the time of the crime, and also that the severity of the impairment would likely have left jurors interpreting his flat demeanor as indicating a callous individual.

The prosecutor repeatedly depicted Beardslee as a remorseless killer, and told the jury that they could evaluate him from his demeanor in the courtroom. The jury was not presented with the evidence of brain damage, allowing the prosecutor to argue that the defendant was "not suffering from any mental disorder."

Donald Beardslee was executed in California in 2005.

Charles Singleton (Schizophrenia)

Charles Singleton was sentenced to death in 1979 for murder. His mental condition worsened in the years that he was on death row, and he was diagnosed as likely suffering from schizophrenia. Charles Singleton was regularly on anti-psychotic drugs. When he did not take the medication, or he needed increased or different medication, his symptoms would worsen. When his illness became severe, he was put on an involuntary medication regime. His psychotic symptoms abated, and the state set an execution date.

Charles Singleton was executed in Arkansas in 2004.

Kevin Zimmerman (Brain Injury)

Kevin Zimmerman had a history of mental problems beginning after a serious bicycle accident at the age of 11, as a result of which he had a plate put in his head. There were numerous relatives and neighbors who could have testified that his personality and behavior changed after the accident.

In 1997, an expert conducted an evaluation of Kevin Zimmermann, and found that his childhood brain injury had "materially affected his behavioral control, both as an adolescent and at the time of the stabbing." In 1995 another doctor had concluded that Zimmerman showed signs of a mental disorder characterized by impaired impulse control and judgment.

In 2003, a psychologist concluded that Kevin Zimmerman had suffered a "traumatic and serious frontal brain injury at the age of eleven, which resulted in the development of seizures, personality changes, explosive outbursts as well as post-explosive amnesia." She said that due to the mental impairments, the murder for which Zimmerman was sentenced to death "should not be considered as a predatory/premeditated crime." She also concluded that Kevin Zimmerman's "behavior at the time of the crime and around the time of his trial raises the strong probability that he was suffering from a separate mental illness or disorder" at those times.

The lawyers failed to present expert psychiatric evidence as mitigation evidence against the death penalty.

Kevin Zimmerman was executed in Texas in 2004.

Hung Thanh Le (PTSD)

Hung Thanh Le had reportedly witnessed, and was subjected to, violence and deprivation in the refugee camps in Cambodia and Thailand. After the trial, a Vietnamese psychologist concluded that Hung Le was suffering from post-traumatic stress disorder (PTSD) at the time of the crime—the murder of a fellow Vietnamese refugee in Oklahoma City in 1992.

The jury heard no expert evidence of the possible impact of Hung Thanh Le's traumatic refugee experiences on his actions.

Hung Thanh Le was executed in Oklahoma in 2004.

Kelsey Patterson (Paranoid Schizophrenia)

After shooting two people, Kelsey Patterson put down the gun, undressed and was pacing up and down the street in his socks, shouting incomprehensibly, when the police arrived. In 2000, a federal judge wrote:

"Patterson had no motive for the killings—he claims he commits acts involuntarily and outside forces control him through implants in his brain and body. Patterson has consistently maintained he is a victim of an elaborate conspiracy, and his lawyers and his doctors are part of that conspiracy. He refuses to cooperate with either; he has refused to be examined by mental health professionals since 1984, he refuses dental treatment, and he refuses to acknowledge that his lawyers represent him. Because of his lack of cooperation, it has been difficult for mental health professionals to determine with certainty whether he is exaggerating the extent of his delusions, or to determine whether he is incompetent or insane. All of the professionals who have tried to examine him agree that he is mentally ill. The most common diagnosis is paranoid schizophrenia."

Patterson was first diagnosed with schizophrenia in 1981. A jury found him competent to stand trial for the murders. Yet his behavior at his competency hearing, and at the trial itself provided compelling evidence that his delusions did not allow him a rational understanding of what was going on or the ability to consult with his lawyers.

After learning of his execution date, Patterson wrote rambling letters to various officials. In the letters he referred to a permanent stay of execution that he said he had received on grounds of innocence. Kelsey Patterson's family had tried unsuccessfully to get treatment for him prior to his crime.

Kelsey Patterson was executed in Texas in 2004.

Robert Bryan (Paranoid Schizophrenia/Brain Disease)

Robert Bryan had been diagnosed with chronic paranoid schizophrenia, and had a history of organic brain disease that may have been related to his severe diabetes dating back decades.

Despite serious concerns about his competence to stand trial, and the fact that he had previously been found incompetent to stand trial, Robert Bryan's trial lawyer presented no mental health evidence at either stage of the trial.

Robert Bryan was executed in Oklahoma in 2004.

Stephen Vrabel (Paranoid Schizophrenia)

Stephen Vrabel shot his girlfriend and their child in 1989, and then put their bodies in the refrigerator. He was found incompetent to stand trial and he was committed to a psychiatric hospital where he remained for the next five years, until he was found competent to stand trial.

Vrabel was diagnosed with serious mental illness, including paranoid schizophrenia. Three Ohio Supreme Court Justices dissented against his death sentence on the ground of Vrabel's mental illness.

Stephen Vrabel was executed in Ohio in 2004.

Kevin Hocker (Bipolar Disorder)

Kevin Hocker suffered from bipolar disorder. His trial for a 1998 murder lasted one day. The trial lawyer presented no witnesses, and Hocker refused to allow any mitigating evidence to be presented, so the jury was left unaware of the abuse he was subjected to as a child, his history of mental illness, or the fact that his father had also suffered from bipolar disorder and had committed suicide when Hocker was eight years old.

Kevin Hocker refused to appeal his sentence. He mutilated himself on death row, including cutting off his testicles. His mother and sister said that he had been suicidal for years. His sister said that her brother had told her that he committed the crime in order to get the death penalty.

Kevin Hocker was executed in Alabama in 2004.

Mark Bailey (Bipolar Disorder)

Lawyers for Mark Bailey, a former Navy submariner, appealed for clemency from the Governor of Virginia on the grounds that Bailey suffered from bipolar disorder, and had faced "a continuous struggle with his mental illness," a factor which was not considered by the jury when it sentenced him to death for killing his wife and child in 1998.

Mark Bailey was executed in Virginia in 2004.

FALSE CONFESSIONS AND THE MENTALLY IMPAIRED

Studies and surveys have found that the mentally impaired are more likely to make false confessions, in part because they are more vulnerable to suggestion. A recent study conducted by a Northwestern University law professor and a criminologist examined 125 cases in which individuals were exonerated after giving false confessions. The researchers found that 22% of the cases involved individuals with mental retardation.

According to a study conducted by an Emory University professor, mentally impaired individuals are more likely to go along, agree and comply with authority figures—i.e., to say what the police want them to say—than the general population." The study that found that the mentally impaired—even those with mild forms of mental retardation—are largely incapable of understanding police admonitions of their right to remain silent and to have an attorney.

According to a study published in the University of Chicago Law Review, only 27% of disabled persons understood that confessions can be used against a suspect, while 91% of non-disabled persons understood this concept. Disabled subjects were also found to be far less likely to understand that police cannot threaten suspects, that police and judges cannot force suspects to talk, and that there is no penalty for remaining silent.

CHAPTER 8:
SENTENCE REVIEW

IN GENERAL

Once there has been a guilty verdict, the defendant loses the presumption of innocence. The appeal then focuses on the procedures that led to that guilty verdict. Federal courts reviewing a state capital case only review constitutional violations and do not consider new factual evidence pointing to innocence.

Most states require any new evidence of innocence to be produced within a set time limitation for consideration on appeal. Ideally, evidence of innocence should be uncovered before the defendant is convicted and sentenced to death. However, due to inadequate counsel and limited resources, this is often not the case. Unfortunately, if that evidence comes too late, it will often be rejected on technical procedural grounds, no matter how strongly it proves the defendant's innocence.

Since the death penalty was reinstated in 1976, a majority of capital convictions have been overturned, primarily due to incompetent legal counsel, erroneous juror instructions, and suppression of exculpatory evidence.

Between 1973 and 1995, seven percent of those prisoners whose sentences were overturned were acquitted, and ten percent were retried and re-sentenced to death. In the remaining cases that were overturned, the prisoners typically ended up with lesser sentences, up to and including life imprisonment.

AUTOMATIC REVIEW

Almost all states provide for automatic review of all death sentences regardless of the defendant's wishes. In South Carolina the defendant has the right to waive sentence review if he or she is deemed competent by the court.

The state's highest appellate court usually conducts the review. If either the conviction or sentence is vacated, the case could be remanded to the trial court for additional proceedings or retrial. As a result of retrial or resentencing, a death sentence could be reimposed.

While most states authorize an automatic review of both the conviction and sentence, Idaho, Indiana, Kentucky, Oklahoma, and Tennessee require review of the sentence only.

In Arkansas, case law provides that the Supreme Court review the trial court record for error in capital cases. Such a review is independent of a defendant's right to waive appeals.

In Idaho, review of the conviction has to be filed through appeal or forfeited.

In Indiana and Kentucky, a defendant could waive review of the conviction.

In Virginia, a defendant could waive an appeal of trial court error but could not waive review of the death sentence for arbitrariness and proportionality.

In Mississippi, the question of whether the defendant could waive the right to automatic review had not been addressed.

In Wyoming, neither statute nor case law precludes a waiver of appeal.

There are no automatic review provisions under the federal death penalty procedures.

FEDERAL HABEAS CORPUS REVIEW OF STATE CRIMINAL CONVICTIONS

In General

State prisoners can challenge the validity of their convictions and sentences by filing habeas corpus petitions in a federal court. These petitions allege that the police, prosecutor, defense counsel, or trial court deprived the prisoners of their federal constitutional rights, such as the right to refuse to answer questions when placed in police custody, the right to a speedy and fair trial, and the right to effective assistance of counsel.

For the past several years, the number of habeas corpus petitions filed in federal district courts has equaled or slightly exceeded 10,000 cases—constituting 4% of the entire federal district court civil caseload.

Most prisoners who have filed the habeas corpus petitions were convicted of violent crimes—e.g., homicide—and were given a correspondingly severe sentence. More than 21% of those prisoners received a life sentence, including life with parole, life without parole, and life plus an additional number of years. Less than 1% of the sentences were death-penalty sentences.

Because these petitions must be presented to the state courts for review, the prisoners are relitigating previously resolved issues. Nevertheless, if these petitions are successful in federal courts, federal judges can issue writs of habeas corpus ordering the prisoners to be released from custody, their sentences reduced, or their cases remanded for retrial or resentencing.

Jurisdiction

Although a state's appellate court may have expended considerable time and resources in reviewing a conviction and/or sentence, lower federal courts still have jurisdiction to review the state court criminal proceedings for possible violations of federal constitutional provisions. Federal jurisdiction has been granted both by statute (28 U.S.C. 2241) and case law (*Brown v. Allen,* 344 U.S. 443 (1953)). Nevertheless, according to the Bureau of Justice Statistics, very few petitions are granted. Thus, the validity of state court convictions remains relatively undisturbed.

If the petition is successful in federal court, the federal judge is empowered to issue a writ of habeas corpus directing certain relief, e.g., that the prisoner be released from custody, that the sentence be reduced, or that the case be remanded for retrial or resentencing.

Case Processing Time

Case processing times vary considerably, with the fastest 10% taking less than a month to resolve and the slowest 10% taking over 2 years to resolve, depending on the number and complexity of the issues. The greater the number of issues in the petition, the longer the time it takes to resolve the petition.

In addition, other factors related to case complexity, such as the appointment of counsel and the holding of evidentiary hearings, increase case processing time. Case processing time is affected only to a limited extent by case characteristics, e.g., the most serious offense at conviction; the underlying trial court proceeding; the sentence; and the type of issue. Thus, the Federal review appears to be an efficient process shaped by relevant legal factors.

Prisoners with relatively short sentences—i.e., five years or less—are likely to be released before their habeas corpus proceedings have resolved.

Representation

The majority of habeas corpus petitions are brought by prisoners acting "pro se"—i.e., as their own attorney. A small percentage of prisoners are either represented by privately retained lawyers, assigned counsel, the ACLU, or some other anti-death penalty organization.

Although there is no constitutional right to an attorney in civil litigation, the court will generally request private attorneys to represent a prisoner when the legal issues are complex and an evidentiary hearing might be necessary.

Types of Issues Raised in Habeas Corpus Petitions

As set forth below, the issue most frequently raised in a habeas corpus petition is that the prisoner received ineffective assistance of counsel, such as the defense counsel not cross-examining a prosecution witness or not objecting to a denial of the court's continuance motion. Fewer issues claim constitutional violations by the trial court, prosecutor, or the police.

According to the Bureau of Justice Statistics, the following issues are typically raised in habeas corpus petitions:

1. Ineffective assistance of counsel (25%)

2. Trial court errors (15%)

3. Fourteenth Amendment issues (14%)

4. Fifth Amendment issues (12%)

5. Sixth Amendment issues (7%)

6. Eighth Amendment issues (7%)

7. Prosecutorial misconduct (6%)

8. Fourth Amendment issues (5%)

9. Miscellaneous other issues (9%)

Generally, the issues raised were primarily focused on the conduct of defense counsel and the state trial court judge, rather than on the prosecutor's behavior.

Dismissal of the Petition

A petition may be dismissed, however, if it fails to meet the procedural requirements of habeas corpus. For example, prisoners must file a direct appeal in the state court for review before they are permitted to file a habeas corpus petition in the federal court. This is known as the "exhaustion doctrine" because the prisoner is required to "exhaust" all state remedies before proceeding to the federal level. As set forth below, this ground accounts for the majority of dismissals.

According to the Bureau of Justice Statistics, habeas corpus petitions are generally dismissed on the following grounds:

1. Failure to exhaust State remedies (57%)

2. Procedural fault (12%)

3. Failure to meet court deadlines or court rules (7%)

4. Issues not cognizable (6%)

5. Abuse of the writ (5%)

6. Government's motion to dismiss granted (4%)

7. Prisoner not in custody (3%)

8. Successive petition (3%)

9. Jurisdictional bar (1%)

10. Petition is moot (1%)

11. Other reasons, e.g., prisoner moves to dismiss petition (3%)

CLEMENCY

Authority to Grant Clemency

In federal cases, only the President of the United States has pardon power. Among the states, the clemency process varies, but typically involves the governor and/or a board of advisors.

In the following states, the governor has sole authority to grant clemency: Alabama, California, Colorado, Kansas, Kentucky, New Mexico, North Carolina, Oregon, South Carolina, Virginia, Washington, and Wyoming.

In the following states, the governor must have the recommendation of clemency from a board or advisory group: Arizona, Delaware, Florida, Louisiana, Montana, Oklahoma, Pennsylvania, and Texas.

In the following states, the governor may receive a non-binding recommendation of clemency from a board or advisory group: Arkansas, Illinois, Indiana, Maryland, Mississippi, Missouri, New Hampshire, Ohio, South Dakota, and Tennessee.

In Connecticut, Georgia, and Idaho, a board or advisory group determines clemency. In Nebraska, Nevada, and Utah, the governor sits on a board or advisory group that determines clemency.

A Directory of State Governors' Offices may be found in Appendix 20 of this Almanac.

Recent Cases

According to the Death Penalty Information Center, since the death penalty was reinstated in 1976, 241 death row inmates have been granted clemency for humanitarian reasons. Humanitarian reasons include doubts about the defendant's guilt or conclusions of the governor regarding the death penalty process. Following are some of the most recent cases where clemency was granted:

John Spirko

In January 2008, Ohio Governor Ted Strickland reduced John Spirko's death sentence to life without parole. In his statement granting clemency, the governor cited "the lack of physical evidence linking him to the murder, as well as the slim residual doubt about his responsibility for the murder that arises from careful scrutiny of the case record."

Jeffrey Leonard

In December 2007, Kentucky Governor Ernie Fletcher commuted Leonard's death sentence to life in prison without parole. Fletcher said Leonard was not provided adequate representation by his attorney, who has admitted he didn't even know Leonard's name during the trial.

Michael Boyd

In September 2007, Tennessee Governor Phil Bredesen commuted the death sentence of Boyd, to life in prison without parole, citing ineffective legal counsel at his sentencing and procedural limitations on his appeals.

Kenneth Foster

In August 2007, Texas Governor Rick Perry commuted the death sentence of Foster to life in prison without parole, expressing concern about the Texas law that allows capital murder defendants to be tried simultaneously.

Robin Lovitt

In November 2005, Virginia Governor Mark Warner commuted the death sentence of Lovitt to life in prison without parole because a state court clerk had illegally destroyed evidence from Lovitt's trial that could have been used in his appeals.

Arthur P. Baird II

In August 2005, Indiana Governor Mitch Daniels commuted the death sentence of Baird, who is severely mentally ill, to life in prison without parole, because that sentence was not available at the time of Baird's sentencing and many of the jurors in the trial and the family of the victims believe that Baird deserved life without parole due to his mental illness.

Michael Daniels

In January 2005, Indiana Governor Joe Kernan commuted the death sentence of Daniels to life in prison without parole because of doubts about Daniels' personal responsibility for the crime and the quality of legal process leading to his death sentence.

Broad Clemencies

Since 1976, there have been four broad grants of clemency to death row inmates:

1. In 1986, former New Mexico Governor Toney Anaya granted clemency to all inmates.

2. In 1991, former Ohio Governor Richard Celeste granted clemency to 8 inmates.

3. In 2003, former Illinois Governor George Ryan granted clemency to all inmates.

4. In 2007, New Jersey Governor Jon Corzine granted clemency to all inmates.

APPENDIX 1:
THE FLORIDA DEATH PENALTY STATUTE

FLORIDA STATUTES (1993)

SEC. 921.141 Sentence of death or life imprisonment for capital felonies; further proceedings to determine sentence.

(1) SEPARATE PROCEEDINGS ON ISSUE OF PENALTY.

Upon conviction or adjudication of guilt of a defendant of a capital felony, the court shall conduct a separate sentencing proceeding to determine whether the defendant should be sentenced to death or life imprisonment as authorized by §. 775.082. The proceeding shall be conducted by the trial judge before the trial jury as soon as practicable. If, through impossibility or inability, the trial jury is unable to reconvene for a hearing on the issue of penalty, having determined the guilt of the accused, the trial judge may summon a special juror or jurors as provided in chapter 913 to determine the issue of the imposition of the penalty. If the trial jury has been waived, or if the defendant pleaded guilty, the sentencing proceeding shall be conducted before a jury impaneled for that purpose, unless waived by the defendant. In the proceeding, evidence may be presented as to any matter that the court deems relevant to the nature of the crime and the character of the defendant and shall include matters relating to any of the aggravating or mitigating circumstances enumerated in subsections (5) and (6). Any such evidence which the court deems to have probative value may be received, regardless of its admissibility under the exclusionary rules of evidence, provided the defendant is accorded a fair opportunity to rebut any hearsay statements. However, this subsection shall not be construed to authorize the introduction of any evidence secured in violation of the Constitution of the United States or the Constitution of the State of Florida. The state and the defendant or his counsel shall be permitted to present argument for or against sentence of death.

(2) ADVISORY SENTENCE BY THE JURY.

After hearing all the evidence, the jury shall deliberate and render an advisory sentence to the court, based upon the following matters:

(a) Whether sufficient aggravating circumstances exist as enumerated in subsection (5);

(b) Whether sufficient mitigating circumstances exist which outweigh the aggravating circumstances found to exist; and

(c) Based on these considerations, whether the defendant should be sentenced to life imprisonment or death.

(3) FINDINGS IN SUPPORT OF SENTENCE OF DEATH.

Notwithstanding the recommendation of a majority of the jury, the court, after weighing the aggravating and mitigating circumstances, shall enter a sentence of life imprisonment or death, but if the court imposes a sentence of death, it shall set forth in writing its findings upon which the sentence of death is based as to the facts:

(a) That sufficient aggravating circumstances exist as enumerated in subsection (5), and

(b) That there are insufficient mitigating circumstances to outweigh the aggravating circumstances.

In each case in which the court imposes the death sentence, the determination of the court shall be supported by specific written findings of fact based upon the circumstances in subsections (5) and (6) and upon the records of the trial and the sentencing proceedings. If the court does not make the findings requiring the death sentence, the court shall impose sentence of life imprisonment in accordance with § 775.082.

(4) REVIEW OF JUDGMENT AND SENTENCE.

The judgment of conviction and sentence of death shall be subject to automatic review by the Supreme Court of Florida within 60 days after certification by the sentencing court of the entire record, unless the time is extended for an additional period not to exceed 30 days by the Supreme Court for good cause shown. Such review by the Supreme Court shall have priority over all other cases and shall be heard in accordance with rules promulgated by the Supreme Court.

(5) AGGRAVATING CIRCUMSTANCES.

Aggravating circumstances shall be limited to the following:

(a) The capital felony was committed by a person under sentence of imprisonment or placed on community control.

(b) The defendant was previously convicted of another capital felony or of a felony involving the use or threat of violence to the person.

(c) The defendant knowingly created a great risk of death to many persons.

(d) The capital felony was committed while the defendant was engaged, or was an accomplice, in the commission of, or an attempt to commit, or flight after committing or attempting to commit, any robbery, sexual battery, arson, burglary, kidnapping, or aircraft piracy or the unlawful throwing, placing, or discharging of a destructive device or bomb.

(e) The capital felony was committed for the purpose of avoiding or preventing a lawful arrest or effecting an escape from custody.

(f) The capital felony was committed for pecuniary gain.

(g) The capital felony was committed to disrupt or hinder the lawful exercise of any governmental function or the enforcement of laws.

(h) The capital felony was especially heinous, atrocious, or cruel.

(i) The capital felony was a homicide and was committed in a cold, calculated, and premeditated manner without any pretense of moral or legal justification.

(j) The victim of the capital felony was a law enforcement officer engaged in the performance of his official duties.

(k) The victim of the capital felony was an elected or appointed public official engaged in the performance of his official duties if the motive for the capital felony was related, in whole or in part, to the victim's official capacity.

(6) MITIGATING CIRCUMSTANCES.

Mitigating circumstances shall be the following:

(a) The defendant has no significant history of prior criminal activity.

(b) The capital felony was committed while the defendant was under the influence of extreme mental or emotional disturbance.

(c) The victim was a participant in the defendant's conduct or consented to the act.

(d) The defendant was an accomplice in the capital felony committed by another person and his participation was relatively minor.

(e) The defendant acted under extreme duress or under the substantial domination of another person.

(f) The capacity of the defendant to appreciate the criminality of his conduct or to conform his conduct to the requirements of law was substantially impaired.

(g) The age of the defendant at the time of the crime.

(7) VICTIM IMPACT EVIDENCE.

Once the prosecution has provided evidence of the existence of one or more aggravating circumstances as described in subsection (5), the prosecution may introduce, and subsequently argue, victim impact evidence. Such evidence shall be designed to demonstrate the victim's uniqueness as an individual human being and the resultant loss to the community's members by the victim's death. Characterizations and opinions about the crime, the defendant, and the appropriate sentence shall not be permitted as a part of victim impact evidence.

(8) APPLICABILITY.

This section does not apply to a person convicted or adjudicated guilty of a capital drug trafficking felony under § 893.135.

APPENDIX 2:
TABLE OF NUMBER OF PRISONERS
EXECUTED IN 2007, BY STATE

STATE	NUMBER OF EXECUTIONS
Alabama	3
Alaska	2
Arizona	1
Arkansas	0
California	0
Colorado	0
Connecticut	0
Delaware	0
District of Columbia	0
Florida	0
Georgia	1
Hawaii	0
Idaho	0
Illinois	0
Indiana	0
Iowa	0
Kansas	0
Kentucky	0

STATE	NUMBER OF EXECUTIONS
Louisiana	0
Maine	0
Maryland	0
Massachusetts	0
Michigan	0
Minnesota	0
Mississippi	0
Missouri	0
Montana	0
Nebraska	0
Nevada	0
New Hampshire	0
New Jersey	0
New Mexico	0
New York	0
North Carolina	0
North Dakota	0
Ohio	2
Oklahoma	3
Oregon	0
Pennsylvania	0
Rhode Island	0
South Carolina	1
South Dakota	1
Tennessee	2
Texas	26
Utah	0
Vermont	0
Virginia	0

STATE	NUMBER OF EXECUTIONS
Washington	0
West Virginia	0
Wisconsin	0
Wyoming	0
Total U.S. Executions	**42**

Source: Bureau of Justice Statistics.

APPENDIX 3:
TABLE OF NUMBER OF PRISONERS UNDER SENTENCE OF DEATH (FEDERAL/STATE) AS OF DECEMBER 31, 2006

STATE	NUMBER OF PRISONERS
Alabama	201
Alaska	0
Arizona	114
Arkansas	38
California	669
Colorado	1
Connecticut	9
Delaware	19
District of Columbia	0
Florida	388
Georgia	107
Hawaii	0
Idaho	19
Illinois	13
Indiana	20

STATE	NUMBER OF PRISONERS
Iowa	0
Kansas	10
Kentucky	39
Louisiana	85
Maine	0
Maryland	5
Massachusetts	0
Michigan	0
Minnesota	0
Mississippi	65
Missouri	45
Montana	2
Nebraska	10
Nevada	83
New Hampshire	0
New Jersey	0
New Mexico	1
New York	0
North Carolina	166
North Dakota	0
Ohio	186
Oklahoma	82
Oregon	35
Pennsylvania	228
Rhode Island	0
South Carolina	58
South Dakota	3
Tennessee	96
Texas	370

STATE	NUMBER OF PRISONERS
Utah	10
Vermont	0
Virginia	20
Washington	8
West Virginia	0
Wisconsin	0
Wyoming	2
Federal	50
U.S. Military	6
Total	3,350

Source: Bureau of Justice Statistics.

APPENDIX 4:
TABLE OF NUMBER OF PRISONERS UNDER SENTENCE OF DEATH, BY YEAR (1953–2006)

YEAR	NUMBER OF PRISONERS
1953	131
1954	147
1955	125
1956	146
1957	151
1958	147
1959	164
1960	212
1961	257
1962	267
1963	297
1964	315
1965	331
1966	406
1967	435
1968	517
1969	575

YEAR	NUMBER OF PRISONERS
1970	631
1971	642
1972	334
1973	134
1974	244
1975	488
1976	420
1977	423
1978	482
1979	593
1980	692
1981	860
1982	1066
1983	1209
1984	1420
1985	1575
1986	1800
1987	1967
1988	2117
1989	2243
1990	2346
1991	2465
1992	2580
1993	2727
1994	2905
1995	3064
1996	3242
1997	3328
1998	3465

YEAR	NUMBER OF PRISONERS
1999	3540
2000	3601
2001	3577
2002	3562
2003	3377
2004	3320
2005	3245
2006	3228

Source: Bureau of Justice Statistics.

APPENDIX 5:
TABLE OF NUMBER OF EXECUTIONS
(1930–2007)

YEAR	NUMBER OF EXECUTIONS
1930	155
1931	153
1932	140
1933	160
1934	168
1935	199
1936	195
1937	147
1938	190
1939	160
1940	124
1941	123
1942	147
1943	131
1944	120
1945	117
1946	131
1947	153
1948	119

YEAR	NUMBER OF EXECUTIONS
1949	119
1950	82
1951	105
1952	83
1953	62
1954	81
1955	76
1956	65
1957	65
1958	49
1959	49
1960	56
1961	42
1962	47
1963	21
1964	15
1965	7
1966	1
1967	2
1968	0
1969	0
1970	0
1971	0
1972	0
1973	0
1974	0
1975	0
1976	0
1977	1
1978	0

YEAR	NUMBER OF EXECUTIONS
1979	2
1980	0
1981	1
1982	2
1983	5
1984	21
1985	18
1986	18
1987	25
1988	11
1989	16
1990	23
1991	14
1992	31
1993	38
1994	31
1995	56
1996	45
1997	74
1998	68
1999	98
2000	85
2001	66
2002	71
2003	65
2004	59
2005	60
2006	53
2007	42

Source: Bureau of Justice Statistics.

APPENDIX 6:
TABLE OF CAPITAL OFFENSES, BY STATE

STATE	CAPITAL OFFENSES
Alabama	Intentional murder with 1 of 18 aggravating factors
Alaska	N/A
Arizona	First degree murder accompanied by at least 1 of 14 aggravating factors
Arkansas	Capital murder with a finding of at least 1 of 10 aggravating circumstances; treason
California	First degree murder with special circumstances; train-wrecking; treason; perjury causing execution
Colorado	First degree murder with at least 1 of 17 aggravating factors; treason; excludes persons determined to be mentally retarded
Connecticut	Capital felony with 8 categories of aggravated homicide
Delaware	First degree murder with at least 1 statutory aggravating circumstance
District of Columbia	N/A
Florida	First degree murder; felony murder; capital drug-trafficking; capital sexual battery
Georgia	Murder; kidnapping with bodily injury or ransom when the victim dies; aircraft hijacking; treason
Hawaii	N/A
Idaho	First degree murder; aggravated kidnapping; perjury resulting in death

STATE	CAPITAL OFFENSES
Illinois	First degree murder with 1 of 21 aggravating circumstances
Indiana	Murder with 16 aggravating circumstances
Iowa	N/A
Kansas	Capital murder with 8 aggravating circumstances
Kentucky	Murder with aggravating factors; kidnapping with aggravating factors
Louisiana	First degree murder; aggravated rape of victim under age 13; treason
Maine	N/A
Maryland	First degree murder, either premeditated or during commission of a felony, provided certain death eligibility requirements are satisfied
Massachusetts	N/A
Michigan	N/A
Minnesota	N/A
Mississippi	Capital murder; aircraft piracy
Missouri	First degree murder
Montana	Capital murder with 1 of 9 aggravating circumstances; aggravated sexual intercourse without consent
Nebraska	First degree murder with a finding of at least 1 of statutorily-defined aggravating circumstances
Nevada	First degree murder with 15 aggravating circumstances
New Hampshire	Six categories of capital murder
New Jersey	Murder by one's own conduct, by solicitation, committed in furtherance of a narcotics conspiracy, or during commission of a crime or terrorism
New Mexico	First degree murder with at least 1 of 7 statutorily-defined aggravating circumstances
New York	First degree murder with 1 of 13 aggravating factors
North Carolina	First degree murder

STATE	CAPITAL OFFENSES
North Dakota	N/A
Ohio	Aggravated murder with at least 1 of 10 aggravating circumstances
Oklahoma	First degree murder in conjunction with a finding of at least 1 of 8 statutorily-defined aggravating circumstances; sex crimes against a child under 14 years of age
Oregon	Aggravated murder
Pennsylvania	First degree murder with 18 aggravating circumstances
Rhode Island	N/A
South Carolina	Murder with 1 of 12 aggravating circumstances; criminal sexual conduct with a minor with 1 of 9 aggravators
South Dakota	First degree murder with 1 of 10 aggravating circumstances
Tennessee	First degree murder with 1 of 15 aggravating circumstances
Texas	Criminal homicide with 1 of 9 aggravating circumstances
Utah	Aggravated murder
Vermont	N/A
Virginia	First degree murder with 1 of 13 aggravating circumstances
Washington	Aggravated first degree murder
West Virginia	N/A
Wisconsin	N/A
Wyoming	First degree murder

Source: Bureau of Justice Statistics.

APPENDIX 7:
TABLE OF FEDERAL CAPITAL OFFENSES, BY STATUTE

STATUTE	CAPITAL OFFENSE
8 U.S.C. § 1342	Murder related to the smuggling of aliens
18 U.S.C. §§ 32–34	Destruction of aircraft, motor vehicles, or related facilities, resulting in death
18 U.S.C. § 36	Murder committed during a drug-related drive-by shooting
18 U.S.C. § 37	Murder committed at an airport serving international civil aviation
18 U.S.C. § 115(b)(3)	Retaliatory murder of a member of the immediate family of a law enforcement official
18 U.S.C. §§ 241–242, 245, 247	Civil rights offenses resulting in death
18 U.S.C. § 351	Murder of a member of Congress, an important executive official, or a Supreme Court justice
18 U.S.C. § 794	Espionage
18 U.S.C. §§ 844(d), (f), (i)	Death resulting from offenses involving transportation of explosives, destruction of government property, or destruction of property related to foreign or interstate commerce
18 U.S.C. § 924(i)	Murder committed by the use of a firearm during a crime of violence or a drug trafficking crime
18 U.S.C. § 930	Murder committed in a federal government facility

STATUTE	CAPITAL OFFENSE
18 U.S.C. § 1091	Genocide
18 U.S.C. § 1111	First degree murder
18 U.S.C. § 1114	Murder of a federal judge or law enforcement official
18 U.S.C. § 1116	Murder of a foreign official
18 U.S.C. § 1118	Murder by a federal prisoner
18 U.S.C. § 1119	Murder of a U.S. national in a foreign country
18 U.S.C. § 1120	Murder by an escaped federal prisoner already sentenced to life imprisonment
18 U.S.C. § 1121	Murder of a state or local law enforcement official or other person aiding in a federal investigation; murder of a state correctional officer
18 U.S.C. § 1201	Murder during a kidnapping
18 U.S.C. § 1203	Murder during a hostage-taking
18 U.S.C. § 1503	Murder of a court officer or juror
18 U.S.C. § 1512	Murder with the intent of preventing testimony by a witness, victim, or informant
18 U.S.C. § 1513	Retaliatory murder of a witness, victim, or informant
18 U.S.C. § 1716	Mailing of injurious articles with intent to kill or resulting in death
18 U.S.C. § 1751	Assassination or kidnapping resulting in the death of the President or Vice-President
18 U.S.C. § 1958	Murder for hire
18 U.S.C. § 1959	Murder involved in a racketeering offense
18 U.S.C. § 1992	Willful wrecking of a train resulting in death
18 U.S.C. § 2113	Bank robbery related murder or kidnapping
18 U.S.C. § 2119	Murder related to a carjacking
18 U.S.C. § 2245	Murder related to rape or child molestation
18 U.S.C. § 2251	Murder related to sexual exploitation of children
18 U.S.C. § 2280	Murder committed during an offense against maritime navigation

STATUTE	CAPITAL OFFENSE
18 U.S.C. § 2281	Murder committed during an offense against a maritime fixed platform
18 U.S.C. § 2332	Terrorist murder of a U.S. national in another country
18 U.S.C. § 2332a	Murder by the use of a weapon of mass destruction
18 U.S.C. § 22340	Murder involving torture
18 U.S.C. § 2381	Treason
21 U.S.C. § 848(e)	Murder related to a continuing criminal enterprise or related murder of a Federal, state or local law enforcement officer
49 U.S.C. §§ 1472–1473	Death resulting from aircraft hijacking

Source: Bureau of Justice Statistics.

APPENDIX 8:
DIRECTORY OF DEATH PENALTY ABOLITIONIST ORGANIZATIONS

ORGANIZATION	WEBSITE
Abolitionist Action Committee	http://www.abolition.org/
ABA Death Penalty Representation Project	http://www.abanet.org/deathpenalty/
ACLU Capital Punishment Project	http://www.aclu.org/capital/index.html
American Friends Service Committee—Criminal Justice Anti-Death Penalty Program	http://www.afsc.org/community/criminal-justice.htm
Amnesty International	http://www.amnestyusa.org/Death_Penalty/
Buddhist Peace Transformative Justice Program	http://www.bpf.org/html/current_projects/transformative_ justice/transformative_ justice.html
Campaign to End the Death Penalty	http://nodeathpenalty.org/content/index.php
Catholics Against Capital Punishment	http://www.cacp.org/
Citizens United for Alternatives to the Death Penalty	http://www.cuadp.org/
Citizens United for the Rehabilitation of Errants (CURE)	http://www.curenational.org/new/index.html
The Constitution Project—Death Penalty Initiative	http://www.constitutionproject.org/deathpenalty/
Death Penalty News & Updates	http://people.smu.edu/rhalperi/

ORGANIZATION	WEBSITE
The Equal Justice Initiative of the Quixote Center	http://www.ejusa.org/
Fellowship of Reconciliation	http://www.forusa.org/
For Whom the Bell Tolls	http://www.curenational.org/~bells/
Innocence Project	http://www.innocenceproject.org/
Innocent and Executed	http://www.democracyinaction.org/
Journey of Hope from Violence to Healing	http://www.journeyofhope.org/pages/index.htm
The Justice Project	http://thejusticeproject.org/
The Lamp of Hope Project	http://www.lampofhope.org/index.html
Murder Victims Families for Reconciliation	http://www.mvfr.org/
Murder Victims Families for Human Rights	http://www.mvfhr.org/
NAACP Legal Defense Fund	http://www.naacpldf.org/
National Coalition to Abolish the Death Penalty	http://www.ncadp.org/
Religious Organizing Against the Death Penalty Project	http://www.deathpenaltyreligious.org/
Southern Center for Human Rights	http://www.schr.org/
Unitarian Universalists for Alternatives to the Death Penalty	http://www.uuadp.org/
United Church of Christ, Justice and Witness Ministries	http://www.ucc.org/justice/
United Methodist Church General Board of Church and Society: Death Penalty	http://www.umc-gbcs.org/
Witness to Innocence	http://www.witnesstoinnocence.org/

APPENDIX 9:
TABLE OF COMPARISON OF MURDER RATES IN DEATH PENALTY STATES WITH MURDER RATES IN NON-DEATH PENALTY STATES (1990–2006)

YEAR	MURDER RATE IN DEATH PENALTY STATES (PER 100,000)	MURDER RATE IN NON-DEATH PENALTY STATES (PER 100,000)	PERCENT DIFFERENCE
1990	9.5	9.16	4%
1991	9.94	9.27	7%
1992	9.51	8.63	10%
1993	9.69	8.81	10%
1994	9.23	7.88	17%
1995	8.59	6.78	27%
1996	7.72	5.37	44%
1997	7.09	5.00	42%
1998	6.51	4.61	41%
1999	5.86	4.59	28%
2000	5.70	4.25	35%
2001	5.82	4.25	37%
2002	5.82	4.27	36%
2003	5.91	4.10	44%

YEAR	MURDER RATE IN DEATH PENALTY STATES (PER 100,000)	MURDER RATE IN NON-DEATH PENALTY STATES (PER 100,000)	PERCENT DIFFERENCE
2004	5.71	4.02	42%
2005	5.87	4.03	46%
2006	5.9	4.22	40%

Source: Federal Bureau of Investigation.

APPENDIX 10:
TABLE OF EXECUTION METHODS, BY STATE

STATE	METHODS OF EXECUTION
Alabama	Electrocution, lethal injection
Alaska	N/A
Arizona	Lethal injection, lethal gas
Arkansas	Electrocution, lethal injection
California	Lethal injection, lethal gas
Colorado	Lethal injection
Connecticut	N/A
Delaware	Lethal injection, hanging
District of Columbia	N/A
Florida	Electrocution, lethal injection
Georgia	Lethal injection
Hawaii	N/A
Idaho	Firing squad, lethal injection
Illinois	Lethal injection
Indiana	Lethal injection
Iowa	N/A
Kansas	Lethal injection
Kentucky	Electrocution, lethal injection

STATE	METHODS OF EXECUTION
Louisiana	Lethal injection
Maine	N/A
Maryland	Gas chamber
Massachusetts	N/A
Michigan	N/A
Minnesota	N/A
Mississippi	Lethal injection
Missouri	Lethal injection, lethal gas
Montana	Lethal injection
Nebraska	Electrocution
Nevada	Lethal injection
New Hampshire	Lethal injection, hanging
New Jersey	Lethal injection
New Mexico	Lethal injection
New York	Lethal injection
North Carolina	Lethal injection
North Dakota	N/A
Ohio	Lethal injection
Oklahoma	Lethal injection, firing squad
Oregon	Lethal injection
Pennsylvania	Lethal injection
Rhode Island	N/A
South Carolina	Electrocution, lethal injection
South Dakota	Lethal injection
Tennessee	Electrocution, lethal injection
Texas	Lethal injection
Utah	Firing squad, lethal injection
Vermont	N/A
Virginia	Electrocution, lethal injection

STATE	METHODS OF EXECUTION
Washington	Hanging, lethal injection
West Virginia	N/A
Wisconsin	N/A
Wyoming	Lethal injection, lethal gas

Source: Bureau of Justice Statistics.

APPENDIX 11:
TABLE OF TOTAL NUMBER OF
EXECUTIONS, BY STATE, AND METHODS
OF EXECUTION (1976–2007)

STATE	TOTAL
Alabama	38
Alaska	0
Arizona	23
Arkansas	27
California	13
Colorado	1
Connecticut	1
Delaware	14
District of Columbia	0
Florida	64
Georgia	40
Hawaii	0
Idaho	1
Illinois	12
Indiana	19
Iowa	0
Kansas	0

STATE	TOTAL
Kentucky	2
Louisiana	27
Maine	0
Maryland	5
Massachusetts	0
Michigan	0
Minnesota	0
Mississippi	8
Missouri	66
Montana	3
Nebraska	3
Nevada	12
New Hampshire	0
New Jersey	0
New Mexico	1
New York	0
North Carolina	43
North Dakota	0
Ohio	26
Oklahoma	86
Oregon	2
Pennsylvania	3
Rhode Island	0
South Carolina	37
South Dakota	1
Tennessee	4
Texas	405
Utah	6
Vermont	0

STATE	TOTAL
Virginia	98
Washington	4
West Virginia	0
Wisconsin	0
Wyoming	1
Federal Government	3
U.S. Military	0
Total U.S. Executions	1099
Total Executions By Lethal Injection	929 (84.5%)
Total Executions By Electrocution	154 (14.0%)
Total Executions By Lethal Gas	11 (1.0%)
Total Executions By Hanging	3 (0.3%)
Total Executions By Firing Squad	2 (0.2%)

Source: Bureau of Justice Statistics.

APPENDIX 12:
TABLE OF STATES THAT HAVE ADOPTED QUALIFICATION STANDARDS FOR ATTORNEYS HANDLING CAPITAL CASES ON BEHALF OF INDIGENT DEFENDANTS

STATE	STATUTE	STANDARDS ADOPTED
Alabama	Ala. Code § 13A-5-54	Any person indicted for a capital felony who is unable to afford a lawyer must be provided with a court appointed attorney who has no less than five years' prior experience in the active practice of criminal law.
Alaska	N/A	N/A
Arizona	Ariz. Rules of Criminal Procedure § 6.5(c)	All criminal appointments must be made taking into account the skill likely to be required in handling a particular case. This rule is not limited to capital appointments.
Arkansas	Ark. Code § 16-87-205 et seq.	Attorneys must be on an approved list of the Capital Conflicts and Appellate office in order to handle capital cases and may not be excluded from the list solely as a result of inexperience.

STATE	STATUTE	STANDARDS ADOPTED
California	Cal. Judicial Administration Standards § 20	Each Court of Appeals shall maintain three lists of qualified attorneys which specify the minimum qualification for the different types of cases. The rule further states that the Supreme Court shall maintain a list of attorneys for appointment in capital appeals. Attorneys appointed in capital appeals must have been in active practice of law for four years in California state courts, or an equivalent experience; must have attended three approved appellate training programs, including one program concerning the death penalty; must have completed seven appellate cases at least one of which was a homicide; and must have submitted two appellant's opening briefs written by the attorney, one of which involves a homicide, for review by the court or administrator.
Colorado	N/A	N/A
Connecticut	N/A	N/A
Delaware	N/A	N.A
District of Columbia	N/A	N.A
Florida	Fla. Statute. § 27.7001	The position of capital collateral representative has been created to represent indigent defendants in capital appeals. The capital collateral representative must have been, for the preceding five years, a member in good standing of the Florida bar.
Georgia	Ga. Code § 17-12-39	No one may be assigned primary responsibility of representing an indigent unless

STATE	STATUTE	STANDARDS ADOPTED
		licensed to practice in Georgia and otherwise competent to counsel and defend a person accused of a crime. Uniform Court Rule 29.8(E) states that cases in which the death penalty is sought shall be assigned only to attorneys of sufficient experience, skill and competence to ensure effective assistance of counsel.
Hawaii	N/A	N/A
Idaho	Idaho Code § 19-856	Only attorneys licensed to practice in Idaho and otherwise competent to defend a person may represent an indigent. This law does not specifically refer to capital cases.
Illinois	N/A	N/A
Indiana	Ind. Criminal Rule 24	The presiding judge in a capital case must appoint two qualified attorneys to represent an indigent defendant. The lead counsel must be an experienced and active trial practitioner with at least five years of criminal litigation experience; have prior experience as lead or co-counsel in no fewer than five felony jury trials which were tried to completion; have prior experience as lead or co-counsel in at least one case in which the death penalty was sought; and have completed within two years prior to appointment at least twelve hours of training in the defense of capital cases in a course approved by the Indiana Public Defender Commission. Co-counsel must be an experienced and active trial practitioner with at least three years of

STATE	STATUTE	STANDARDS ADOPTED
		criminal litigation experience; have prior experience as lead or co-counsel in no fewer than three felony jury trials which were tried to completion; and have completed within two years prior to the appointment at least twelve hours of training in the defense of capital cases in a course approved by the Indiana Public Defender Commission. In addition, appointed counsel for indigent defendants in capital cases must comply with an overall caseload limit.
Iowa	N/A	N/A
Kansas	N/A	N/A
Kentucky	N/A	N/A
Louisiana	La. Supreme Court Rule XXXI	In capital cases with an indigent defendant, the court must appoint no less than two attorneys to represent the defendant, both of whom must be certified by the Louisiana Indigent Defender Board as qualified in capital cases. One attorney shall be designated lead counsel and the other shall be designated associate counsel.
Maine	N/A	N/A
Maryland	N/A	N/A
Massachusetts	N/A	N/A
Michigan	N/A	N/A
Minnesota	N/A	N/A
Mississippi	N/A	N/A
Missouri	N/A	N/A
Montana	N/A	N/A
Nebraska	N/A	N/A

STATE	STATUTE	STANDARDS ADOPTED
Nevada	Nev. Court Rule 250 (IV)A	In a capital case, an attorney appointed to represent an indigent defendant must have skills adequate to represent the defendant with reasonable professional competence. The following are established as minimum requirements: the attorney shall have acted as counsel in no less than seven felony trials, at least two of which involved violent crimes, including one murder case; the attorney shall have previously acted as co-counsel in at least one death penalty trial; and the attorney shall have been licensed to practice law for at least three years.
New Hampshire	N/A	N/A
New Jersey	N/A	N/A
New Mexico	N/A	N/A
New York	N.Y. Session Law § 5(b)	Two attorneys shall be appointed, one as lead counsel and one as associate counsel. The appointments shall be made from a list of four proposed teams of qualified lead and associate counsel provided to the court by the capital defender office.
North Carolina	N.C. Gen. Stat. § 7A-459	No attorney shall be appointed to represent an indigent defendant in a capital case at the trial level unless he or she has a minimum of five years of experience in the general practice of law and has been found by the court or the public defender to be proficient in the field of criminal trial practice. No attorney shall be appointed to represent an indigent defendant in a capital case at the appellate level

STATE	STATUTE	STANDARDS ADOPTED
		unless he or she has a minimum of five years of experience in the general practice of law and has been found by the trial judge or public defender to have a demonstrated proficiency in the field of appellate practice.
North Dakota	N/A	N/A
Ohio	Ohio Common Pleas Court Rule 65	Trial counsel must consist of lead and co-counsel. Lead counsel must have extensive experience as lead counsel in felony cases, including experience in capital cases, as well as other requirements. Co-counsel must have extensive experience in felony jury trials. Two attorneys must also be appointed at the appellate level and must, among other requirements, have specialized training in defending capital cases.
Oklahoma	None	Standards of qualification are set by the Oklahoma Indigent Defense System Board.
Oregon	None	Oregon has adopted standards patterned after the National Legal Aid and Defender's Association Standards for the Appointment and Performance of Counsel in Death Penalty Cases and the ABA's guidelines for the Appointment and Performance of Counsel in Death Penalty Cases. Standard 3.1(E) of Oregon's Qualification Standards for Court-Appointed Counsel to Represent Indigent Persons at State Expense lists the requirements for the appointing of trial counsel in capital cases, and Standard 3.1(l) lists requirements for counsel at the appellate level in capital cases.

STATE	STATUTE	STANDARDS ADOPTED
Pennsylvania	N/A	N/A
Rhode Island	N/A	N/A
South Carolina	N/A	N/A
South Dakota	N/A	N/A
Tennessee	N/A	N/A
Texas	N/A	N/A
Utah	Utah Criminal Rule 8	Appointed counsel for an indigent defendant in a capital case must be proficient in capital cases. To demonstrate proficiency, at least one of the attorneys must have tried to verdict six felony cases within the past four years or twenty-five felony cases total, five of which must have been tried to verdict within the past five years. In addition, at least one of the attorneys must have appeared as counsel or co-counsel in a capital homicide case which was tried to a jury and which went to final verdict. Also, one of the appointed attorneys must have attended and completed within the past five years an approved continuing legal education course dealing with the trial of death penalty cases. Finally, the combined experience of the appointed attorneys must exceed five years in the active practice of law. In capital appeals for indigent defendants, at least one appointed attorney must have served as counsel in at least three felony appeals and at least one attorney must have attended and completed within the past five years an approved continuing legal education course dealing with the trial or appeal of death penalty cases.

STATE	STATUTE	STANDARDS ADOPTED
Vermont	N/A	N/A
Virginia	Va. Code § 19.2-163.8	Must be an active member in good standing of the Virginia State Bar; have extensive experience in litigation or appeals of criminal felonies; and have had specialized training in capital litigation.
Washington	N/A	N/A
West Virginia	N/A	N/A
Wisconsin	N/A	N/A
Wyoming	N/A	N/A

APPENDIX 13:
TABLE OF DEATH ROW PRISONERS
EXONERATED, BY STATE

STATE	NUMBER OF EXONERATIONS
Alabama	5
Arizona	8
California	3
Florida	22
Georgia	5
Idaho	1
Illinois	18
Indiana	2
Kentucky	1
Louisiana	8
Maryland	1
Massachusetts	3
Mississippi	3
Missouri	3
Nebraska	1
Nevada	1
New Mexico	4
North Carolina	6

STATE	NUMBER OF EXONERATIONS
Ohio	5
Oklahoma	8
Pennsylvania	6
South Carolina	2
Tennessee	1
Texas	8
Virginia	1
Washington	1

Source: Death Penalty Information Center.

APPENDIX 14:
TABLE OF DEATH ROW PRISONERS EXONERATED, BY YEAR

YEAR	NUMBER OF EXONERATIONS
1973	1
1974	1
1975	4
1976	4
1977	1
1978	2
1979	1
1980	2
1981	4
1982	2
1983	0
1984	0
1985	1
1986	3
1987	8
1988	2
1989	4
1990	4

YEAR	NUMBER OF EXONERATIONS
1991	3
1992	1
1993	6
1994	1
1995	5
1996	8
1997	6
1998	2
1999	8
2000	9
2001	5
2002	4
2003	12
2004	6
2005	2
2006	1
2007	3
2008	1

Source: Death Penalty Information Center.

APPENDIX 15:
TABLE OF NUMBER OF PRISONERS UNDER SENTENCE OF DEATH, BY RACE (1968–2006)

YEAR	WHITE	BLACK	OTHER
1968	243	271	3
1969	263	310	2
1970	293	335	3
1971	306	332	4
1972	167	166	1
1973	64	68	2
1974	110	128	6
1975	218	262	8
1976	225	195	0
1977	229	192	2
1978	281	197	4
1979	354	236	3
1980	424	264	4
1981	499	353	8
1982	613	441	12
1983	692	505	12
1984	806	598	16

YEAR	WHITE	BLACK	OTHER
1985	896	664	15
1986	1013	762	25
1987	1128	813	26
1988	1235	848	34
1989	1308	898	37
1990	1368	940	38
1991	1449	979	37
1992	1511	1031	38
1993	1575	1111	41
1994	1653	1203	49
1995	1732	1284	48
1996	1833	1358	51
1997	1864	1408	56
1998	1917	1489	59
1999	1960	1515	65
2000	1989	1541	71
2001	1968	1538	71
2002	1939	1551	72
2003	1883	1417	78
2004	1856	1390	74
2005	1802	1366	77
2006	1802	1352	74

Source: Bureau of Justice Statistics.

APPENDIX 16:
TABLE OF NUMBER OF WOMEN PRISONERS UNDER SENTENCE OF DEATH, BY RACE (FEDERAL/STATE) (AS OF DECEMBER 31, 2006)

STATE	WHITE	BLACK	OTHER	TOTAL
Alabama	1	2	0	3
Arizona	2	0	0	2
California	11	2	2	15
Florida	0	0	0	0
Georgia	1	0	0	1
Idaho	1	0	0	1
Illinois	0	0	0	0
Indiana	0	1	0	1
Kentucky	1	0	0	1
Louisiana	1	1	0	2
Mississippi	3	0	0	3
Missouri	0	0	0	0
Nevada	0	0	0	0
North Carolina	2	1	1	4
Ohio	1	0	0	1

STATE	WHITE	BLACK	OTHER	TOTAL
Oklahoma	1	0	0	1
Pennsylvania	2	3	0	5
Tennessee	2	0	0	2
Texas	5	5	0	10
Virginia	1	0	0	1
Federal	1	0	0	1
Total U.S.	36	15	3	54

Source: Bureau of Justice Statistics.

APPENDIX 17:
TABLE OF NUMBER OF PRISONERS
UNDER SENTENCE OF DEATH, BY AGE
(AS OF DECEMBER 31, 2006)

AGE	NUMBER	PERCENTAGE
19 or Younger	0	0
20–24	51	1.6
25–29	280	8.7
30–34	455	14.1
35–39	596	18.5
40–44	563	17.4
45–49	553	17.1
50–54	331	10.3
55–59	246	7.6
60–64	103	3.2
65 or Older	50	1.5

Source: Bureau of Justice Statistics.

APPENDIX 18:
STATUTES DEFINING MENTAL RETARDATION FOR THE PURPOSE OF IMPOSITION OF THE DEATH PENALTY

STATE	STATUTE	DEFINITION OF MENTAL RETARDATION
Alabama	None Listed	None Listed
Arizona	Ariz. Rev. Stat. § 13-3982	A condition based on a mental deficit that has resulted in significantly sub average general intellectual functioning existing concurrently with significant limitations in adaptive functioning, where the onset of the forgoing conditions occurred before the defendant reached the age of eighteen.
Arkansas	Ark. Code § 5-4-618	Significantly sub-average general intellectual functioning accompanied by significant deficits or impairments in adaptive functioning, and manifested in the developmental period. The age of onset is 18. There is a rebuttable presumption of mental retardation when the defendant has an IQ of 65 or below.
California	Cal. Penal Code § 1376	Significantly sub-average general intellectual functioning

STATE	STATUTE	DEFINITION OF MENTAL RETARDATION
		existing concurrently with deficits in adaptive behavior and manifested before the age of 18.
Colorado	Colo. Rev. Stat. § 16-9-401-403	Any defendant with significantly sub-average general intellectual functioning existing concurrently with substantial deficits in adaptive behavior and manifested and documented during the developmental period. The requirements for documentation may be excused by the court upon a finding that extraordinary circumstances exist. The court does not define extraordinary circumstances. The law does not give a numerical IQ level.
Connecticut	Conn. Public Act No. 01-151	Significantly sub-average general intellectual functioning existing concurrently with deficits in adaptive behavior and manifested during the developmental period. (as defined in Conn. Gen. Stat. § 1-1g (2001))
Delaware	Del. Code § 11-4209	"Seriously mentally retarded" or "serious mental retardation" means that an individual has significantly sub-average intellectual functioning that exists concurrently with substantial deficits in adaptive behavior and both the significantly sub-average intellectual functioning and the deficits in adaptive behavior were manifested before the individual became 18 years of age; "Significantly sub-average intellectual functioning" means an intelligent quotient of 70 or below obtained by assessment with 1 or more of the standardized, individually

STATE	STATUTE	DEFINITION OF MENTAL RETARDATION
		administered general intelligence tests developed for the purpose of assessing intellectual functioning; and "Adaptive behavior" means the effectiveness or degree to which the individual meets the standards of personal independence expected of the individual's age group, sociocultural background and community setting, as evidenced by significant limitations in not less than 2 of the following adaptive skill areas: communication, self-care, home living, social skills, use of community resources, self-direction, functional academic skills, work, leisure, health or safety.
Florida	Fla. Stat. § 921.137	Significantly sub-average general intellectual functioning existing concurrently with deficits in adaptive behavior and manifested during the period from conception to age 18.
Georgia	Ga. Code Ann. § 17-7-131(i)	Significantly sub-average intellectual functioning resulting in or associated with impairments in adaptive behavior which manifests during the developmental period.
Idaho	Idaho Code § 19-2515A	"Mentally retarded" means significantly sub-average general intellectual functioning that is accompanied by significant limitations in adaptive functioning in at least two (2) of the following skill areas: communication, self-care, home living, social or interpersonal skills, use of community resources, self-direction,

STATE	STATUTE	DEFINITION OF MENTAL RETARDATION
		functional academic skills, work, leisure, health and safety. The onset of significant sub-average general intelligence functioning and significant limitations in adaptive functioning must occur before age eighteen (18) years. (b) "Significantly sub-average general intellectual functioning" means an intelligence quotient of seventy (70) or below.
Illinois	Ill. Code § 725 ILCS 5/114-15	The mental retardation must have manifested itself by the age of 18. An intelligence quotient (IQ) of 75 or below is presumptive evidence of mental retardation. IQ tests and psychometric tests administered to the defendant must be the kind and type recognized by experts in the field of mental retardation. In order for the defendant to be considered mentally retarded, a low IQ must be accompanied by significant deficits in adaptive behavior in at least 2 of the following skill areas: communication, self-care, social or interpersonal skills, home living, self-direction, academics, health and safety, use of community resources, and work.
Indiana	Ind. Stat. § 35-36-9-1 et seq.	An individual before becoming 22 years of age manifests: (1) significantly sub-average intellectual functioning; and (2) substantial impairment of adaptive behavior that is documented in a court-ordered evaluative report.
Kansas	Kan. Stat. Ann. § 21-4623	An individual having significantly sub-average general intellectual functioning

STATE	STATUTE	DEFINITION OF MENTAL RETARDATION
		to an extent that substantially impairs one's capacity to appreciate the criminality of one's conduct or conform one's conduct to the requirements of law. The statute does not define adaptive behavior or the age of onset. However, Kan. Stat. Ann § 76-12b01 defines these terms. Adaptive behavior refers to the effectiveness of personal independence and social responsibility expected of that person's age, cultural group and community. The age of onset must be prior to 18 years old.
Kentucky	Ky. Rev. Stat. § 532.130-140	A significant sub-average intellectual functioning existing concurrently with substantial deficits in adaptive behavior and manifested during the developmental period. The age of onset is 18 years old. Significantly sub-average general intellectual functioning is defined as an IQ of 70 or below.
Louisiana	2003 LA Acts § 698, Code of Criminal Procedure Article 905.5.1	A disability characterized by significant limitations in both intellectual functioning and adaptive behavior as expressed in conceptual, social, and practical adaptive skills. Onset must have occurred before age 18.
Maryland	Md. Code Ann. Art. 27 § 412	An individual who has significantly sub-average intellectual functioning as evidenced by an IQ of 70 or below on an individually administered IQ test, and impairment in adaptive behavior. The age of onset is before the age of 22.
Mississippi	None Listed	None Listed

STATE	STATUTE	DEFINITION OF MENTAL RETARDATION
Missouri	Mo. Rev. Stat § 565.030	Significantly sub-average general intellectual functioning which originates before age eighteen; and is associated with a significant impairment in adaptive behavior.
Montana	None Listed	None Listed
Nebraska	Neb. Rev. Stat. § 28-105.01	Mental retardation means significantly sub-average general intellectual functioning existing concurrently with deficits in adaptive behavior. An IQ of 70 or below on a reliably administered IQ test shall be presumptive evidence of mental retardation.
Nevada	Nev. Rev. Stat. § 174	Significant sub-average general intellectual functioning which exists concurrently with deficits in adaptive behavior and manifested during the developmental period.
New Hampshire	None Listed	None Listed
New Mexico	N.M. Stat. Ann. § 31-20A-2.1	Mental retardation refers to significantly sub-average general intellectual functioning existing concurrently with deficits in adaptive behavior. An IQ of 70 or below on a reliably administered IQ test shall be presumptive evidence of mental retardation.
North Carolina	2001 N.C. Sess. Law § 346	Significantly sub-average general intellectual functioning (defined as having an IQ of 70 or below), existing concurrently with significant limitations in adaptive functioning (defined as having significant limitations in two or more of the following adaptive skill areas: communication, self-care, home living, social skills, community

STATE	STATUTE	DEFINITION OF MENTAL RETARDATION
		use, self-direction, health and safety, functional academics, leisure skills and work skills) both of which were manifested before the age of 18.
Ohio	None Listed	None Listed
Oklahoma	None Listed	None Listed
Oregon	None Listed	None Listed
Pennsylvania	None Listed	None Listed
South Carolina	None Listed	None Listed
South Dakota	S.D. Codified Laws § 23A-27A-26.1	Mental retardation means significant sub-average general intellectual functioning existing concurrently with substantial related deficits in applicable adaptive skill areas. An IQ exceeding 70 on a reliable standardized measure of intelligence is presumptive evidence that the defendant does not have significant sub-average general intellectual functioning. Mental retardation must have been manifested and documented before the age of 18 years.
Tennessee	Tenn. Code Ann. Tit. 39 Ch. 13 Pt. 2 § 39-13-203	(1) Significantly sub-average general intellectual functioning as evidenced by a functional IQ of 70 or below; (2) deficits in adaptive behavior; (3) the mental retardation must have been manifested during the developmental period or by age 18. The state does not define "deficits in adaptive behavior." The statute clearly provides that adaptive behavior and intellectual functioning are independent criteria.
Texas	None Listed	None Listed

STATE	STATUTE	DEFINITION OF MENTAL RETARDATION
Utah	Utah Code Ann. § 77-15a-101	Significant sub-average general intellectual functioning that results in and exists concurrently with significant deficiencies in adaptive functioning that exist primarily in the areas of reasoning or impulse control, or in both of these areas; and the sub-average general intellectual functioning and the significant deficiencies in adaptive functioning under Subsection (1) are both manifested prior to age 22.
Virginia	Va. Code Ann. §19.2-264.3	"Mentally retarded" means a disability, originating before the age of 18 years, characterized concurrently by (i) significantly sub-average intellectual functioning as demonstrated by performance on a standardized measure of intellectual functioning administered in conformity with accepted professional practice, that is at least two standard deviations below the mean and (ii) significant limitations in adaptive behavior as expressed in conceptual, social and practical adaptive skills.
Washington	Wash. Rev. Code Ann. § 10.95.030	The individual has (1) significantly sub-average general intellectual functioning; (2) existing concurrently with deficits in adaptive behavior; and (3) both significantly sub-average general intellectual functioning and deficits in adaptive behavior were manifested during the developmental period. The age of onset is 18 years of age. The required IQ level is 70 or below.
Wyoming	None Listed	None Listed

STATE	STATUTE	DEFINITION OF MENTAL RETARDATION
Federal Government	18 U.S.C.A. § 3596(c)	In 1994, Congress adopted legislation to ban the execution of individuals with mental retardation. The statute states that a sentence of death shall not be carried out upon a person who has mental retardation. The statute does not define mental retardation, or discuss at what stage in the criminal proceedings the determination of mental retardation must be made. Earlier, Congress had also provided a form of an exemption for this issue in the Anti-Drug Abuse Act of 1988.

APPENDIX 19:
DEFENDANTS WITH MENTAL RETARDATION EXECUTED SINCE THE REINSTATEMENT OF THE DEATH PENALTY

NAME	STATE	RACE	I.Q.	EXECUTION DATE
Arthur F. Goode III	Florida	White	60–63	04/05/84
Ivon Ray Stanley	Georgia	Black	62	07/12/84
James Dupree Henry	Florida	Black	Low 70s	09/20/84
Morris Odell Mason	Virginia	Black	62–66	06/25/85
James Terry Roach	South Carolina	White	69–70	01/10/86
Jerome Bowden	Georgia	Black	59–65	06/24/86
Willie Celestine	Louisiana	White	68–81	07/20/87
John Brogdon	Louisiana	White	Mildly mentally retarded	07/30/87
Horace Dunkins	Alabama	Black	65–69	07/14/89
Alton Waye	Virginia	Black	Probability of mental retardation	08/30/89
Johnny Ray Anderson	Texas	White	70	05/17/90
Dalton Prejean	Louisiana	Black	71–76	05/18/90
Ricky Ray Rector	Arkansas	Black	Mentally retarded due to a lobotomy	01/24/92

NAME	STATE	RACE	I.Q.	EXECUTION DATE
Johnny Frank Garrett	Texas	Shige	Mentally retarded/ mentally ill	02/11/92
Billy Wayne White	Texas	Black	66–69	04/23/92
Nollie Lee Martin	Florida	White	Mentally retarded/ mentally ill	05/12/92
Ricky Lee Grubbs	Missouri	White	72	10/21/92
Cornelius Singleton	Alabama	Black	55–67	11/20/92
Robert Wayne Sawyer	Louisiana	White	65–68	03/05/93
William Henry Mance	Georgia	Black	Mildly mentally retarded	03/31/94
Mario Marquez	Texas	Latin	65	01/17/95
Willie Clisby	Alabama	Black	Mildly mentally retarded	04/28/95
Varnell Weeks	Alabama	Black	Mildly mentally retarded	05/12/95
Girvies Davis	Illinois	Black	Low borderline mentally retarded	05/17/95
Sylvester Adams	South Carolina	Black	65–69	08/18/95
Barry Lee Fairchild	Arkansas	Black	60–63	08/31/95
Walter Milton Corell	Virginia	White	68	01/04/96
Luis Mata	Arizona	Latin	68–70	08/22/96
John Earl Bush	Florida	Black	Low borderline mentally retarded	10/21/96
Frank Middleton	South Carolina	Black	68–69	11/22/96
Terry Washington	Texas	Black	58–69	05/06/97
Tony Mackall	Virginia	Black	64	02/20/98
Reginald Mackall	Missouri	Black	65	02/25/98
Robert Carter	Texas	Black	Mildly mentally retarded	05/18/98

NAME	STATE	RACE	I.Q.	EXECUTION DATE
Dwayne Allen Wright	Virginia	Black	Mentally retarded/ mentally ill	10/14/98
Ronald Yeats	Virginia	White	70	04/29/99
Norman Lee Newsted	Oklahoma	White	Mentally retarded/ mentally ill	07/08/99
Raymond James Jones	Texas	Black	Mentally retarded	09/01/99
David R. Leisure	Missouri	White	74	09/01/99
Charles Anthony Boyd	Texas	Black	64	08/05/99
Willie Sullivan	Delaware	Black	58–70	09/24/99
Oliver Cruz	Texas	Latin	64–76	08/09/00
Wanda Jean Allen	Oklahoma	Black	69	01/11/00
Robert Clayton	Oklahoma	White	68	03/01/01

APPENDIX 20:
DIRECTORY OF STATE
GOVERNORS' OFFICES

STATE	WEBSITE
Alabama	www.governor.state.al.us
Alaska	www.state.ak.us
Arizona	www.governor.state.az.us
Arkansas	www.accessarkansas.org/governor/
California	www.governor.ca.gov
Colorado	www.colorado.gov/governor/
Connecticut	www.ct.gov/governor/
Delaware	www.state.de.us/governor/
Florida	www.flgov.com/
Georgia	http://gov.state.ga.us/
Hawaii	www.hawaii.gov/gov/
Idaho	www.state.id.us
Illinois	www.illinois.gov/gov/
Indiana	www.state.in.us/gov/
Iowa	www.governor.state.ia.us
Kansas	www.ksgovernor.org
Kentucky	www.governor.ky.gov
Louisiana	www.gov.state.la.us

STATE	WEBSITE
Maine	www.state.me.us/governor/
Maryland	www.gov.state.md.us
Massachusetts	www.mass.gov
Michigan	www.michigan.gov/gov
Minnesota	www.governor.state.mn.us
Mississippi	www.governorbarbour.com
Missouri	www.gov.state.mo.us
Montana	http://governor.mt.gov/
Nebraska	http://gov.nol.org/
Nevada	http://gov.state.nv.us/
New Hampshire	www.state.nh.us/governor/
New Jersey	www.state.nj.us/governor/
New Mexico	www.governor.state.nm.us
New York	www.state.ny.us/governor/
North Carolina	www.governor.state.nc.us
North Dakota	www.governor.state.nd.us
Ohio	http://governor.ohio.gov/
Oklahoma	www.gov.ok.gov
Oregon	www.governor.state.or.us
Pennsylvania	www.state.pa.us/governor/
Rhode Island	www.governor.state.ri.us
South Carolina	www.scgovernor.com
South Dakota	www.state.sd.us/governor/
Tennessee	www.state.tn.us/governor/
Texas	www.governor.state.tx.us
Utah	www.utah.gov/governor/
Vermont	www.vermont.gov/governor/
Virginia	www.governor.virginia.gov
Washington	www.governor.wa.gov

STATE	WEBSITE
West Virginia	www.wvgov.org
Wisconsin	www.wisgov.state.wi.us
Wyoming	http://wyoming.gov/governor/

GLOSSARY

Abolish—To repeal or revoke, such as a law or custom.

Abstention—A policy adopted by the federal courts whereby the district court may decline to exercise its jurisdiction and defer to a state court the resolution of a federal constitutional question, pending the outcome in a state court proceeding.

Abuse of Discretion—A standard of review.

Abuse of Process—The improper and malicious use of the criminal or civil process.

Accusation—An indictment, presentment, information or any other form in which a charge of a crime or offense can be made against an individual.

Accusatory Instrument—The initial pleading that forms the procedural basis for a criminal charge, such as an indictment.

Accuse—To directly and formally institute legal proceedings against a person, charging that he or she has committed an offense.

Acquit—A verdict of "not guilty" which determines that the person is absolved of the charge and prevents a retrial pursuant to the doctrine of double jeopardy.

Acquittal—One who is acquitted receives an acquittal.

Adjourn—To briefly postpone or delay a court proceeding.

Adjudication—The determination of a controversy and pronouncement of judgment.

Admissible Evidence—Evidence that may be received by a trial court to assist the trier of fact, either the judge or jury, in deciding a dispute.

Admission—In criminal law, the voluntary acknowledgment that certain facts are true.

Adversary—Opponent or litigant in a legal controversy or litigation.

Adversary Proceeding—A proceeding involving a real controversy contested by two opposing parties.

Affirmative Defense—In a pleading, a matter constituting a defense.

Amend—As in a pleading, to make an addition to, or a subtraction from, an already existing pleading.

American Bar Association (ABA)—A national organization of lawyers and law students.

American Civil Liberties Union (ACLU)—A nationwide organization dedicated to the enforcement and preservation of rights and civil liberties guaranteed by the federal and state constitutions.

Amnesty—A pardon that excuses one of a criminal offense.

Appeal—Resort to a higher court for the purpose of obtaining a review of a lower court decision.

Appellate Court—A court having jurisdiction to review the law as applied to a prior determination of the same case.

Arraign—In a criminal proceeding, to accuse one of committing a wrong.

Arraignment—The initial step in the criminal process when the defendant is formally charged with the wrongful conduct.

Arrest—To deprive a person of his liberty by legal authority.

Bill of Rights—The first eight amendments to the United States Constitution.

Capital Crime—A crime for which the death penalty may, but need not necessarily, be imposed.

Capital Offense—A criminal offense punishable by death.

Capital Punishment—The penalty of death.

Confession—In criminal law, an admission of guilt or other incriminating statement made by the accused.

Conflict of Law—The body of law by which the court in which the action is pending chooses which law to apply in a controversy, where there exists diversity between the applicable law of two jurisdictions, both of which have an interest.

Confrontation Clause—A sixth Amendment right of the Constitution that permits the accused in a criminal prosecution to confront the witness against him.

Consent Search—A search that is carried out with the voluntary authorization of the subject of the search.

Conspiracy—A scheme by two or more persons to commit a criminal or unlawful act.

Conspirator—One of the parties involved in a conspiracy.

Constitution—The fundamental principles of law that frame a governmental system.

Constitutional Right—Refers to the individual liberties granted by the constitution of a state or the federal government.

Court—The branch of government responsible for the resolution of disputes arising under the laws of the government.

Criminal Court—The court designed to hear prosecutions under the criminal laws.

Cross-Examination—The questioning of a witness by someone other than the one who called the witness to the stand concerning matters about which the witness testified during direct examination.

Cruel and Unusual Punishment—Refers to punishment that is shocking to the ordinary person, inherently unfair, or excessive in comparison to the crime committed.

Disclosure—Disclosure is the act of disclosing or revealing that which is secret or not fully understood.

Discovery—Modern pretrial procedure by which one party gains information held by another party.

Disposition—The process by which the juvenile court decides what is to be done with, for, or about the child who has been found to be within its jurisdiction.

District Attorney—An officer of a governmental body with the duty to prosecute those accused of crimes.

Docket—A list of cases on the court's calendar.

Double Jeopardy—Fifth Amendment provision providing that an individual shall not be subject to prosecution for the same offense more than one time.

Due Process Rights—All rights that are of such fundamental importance as to require compliance with due process standards of fairness and justice.

Entrapment—In criminal law, refers to the use of trickery by the police to induce the defendant to commit a crime for which he or she has a predisposition to commit.

Ex Post Facto—Latin for "after the fact."

Exclusionary Rule—A constitutional rule of law providing that evidence procured by illegal police conduct, although otherwise admissible, will be excluded at trial.

Eyewitness—A person who can testify about a matter because of his or her own presence at the time of the event.

Fact Finder—In a judicial or administrative proceeding, the person, or group of persons, that has the responsibility of determining the acts relevant to decide a controversy.

Fact Finding—A process by which parties present their evidence and make their arguments to a neutral person, who issues a nonbinding report based on the findings that usually contains a recommendation for settlement.

False Arrest—An unlawful arrest.

False Imprisonment—Detention of an individual without justification.

Federal Courts—The courts of the United States.

Felony—A crime of a graver or more serious nature than those designated as misdemeanors.

Felony Murder—A first-degree murder charge that results when a homicide occurs during the course of certain specified felonies, such as arson and robbery.

Grand Jury—A group of people summoned to court to investigate a crime and hand down an indictment if sufficient evidence is presented to hold the accused for trial.

Habeas Corpus—Latin for "You have the body." Refers to a procedure brought by writ to determine the legality of an individual's custody.

Halfway House—A residence where individuals who have been released from a very structured environment, such as a mental institution or prison, are supervised and taught to readjust to society.

Harmless Error—An error committed by a lower court proceeding that does not substantially violate an appellant's rights to an extent, that the lower court proceeding should be modified or overturned.

Hearing—A proceeding during which evidence is taken for the purpose of determining the facts of a dispute and reaching a decision.

Homicide—The killing of a human being by another human being.

Hung Jury—A jury that cannot render a verdict because its members cannot reconcile their differences to a necessary standard, e.g., unanimity, substantial majority.

Illegal—Against the law.

Imprisonment—The confinement of an individual, usually as punishment for a crime.

In Formal Pauperis—Latin for "in the manner of a pauper." It refers to the right of a party to proceed with a lawsuit without costs or certain formalities.

Indictment—A formal written accusation of criminal charges submitted to a grand jury for investigation and indorsement.

Indigent—A person who is financially destitute.

Infancy—The state of a person who is under the age of legal majority.

Infancy Presumption—In common law, the conclusive presumption that children under the age of seven are without criminal capacity.

Inference—A reasoned deduction based on the given facts.

Information—A written accusation of a crime submitted by the prosecutor to inform the accused and the court of the charges and the facts of the crime.

Informer—An individual who gives information concerning criminal activities to governmental authorities on a confidential basis.

Insufficient Evidence—The judicial decision that the evidence submitted to prove a case does not meet the degree necessary to go forward with the action.

Jail—Place of confinement where a person in custody of the government awaits trial or serves a sentence after conviction.

Jailhouse Lawyer—An inmate who gains knowledge of the law through self-study, and assists fellow inmates in preparation of appeals, although he or she is not licensed to practice law.

Judge—The individual who presides over a court, and whose function it is to determine controversies.

Jurisdiction—The power to hear and determine a case.

Jury Trial—A trial during which the evidence is presented to a jury so that they can determine the issues of fact, and render a verdict based upon the law as it applies to their findings of fact.

Legal Aid—A national organization established to provide legal services to those who are unable to afford private representation.

Lineup—A police procedure whereby a suspect is placed in line with other persons of similar description so that a witness to the crime may attempt an identification.

Malicious Prosecution—A cause of action against those who prosecuted unsuccessful civil or criminal actions with malicious intent.

Manslaughter—The unlawful taking of another's life without malice aforethought.

Minor—A person who has not yet reached the age of legal competence, which is designated as 18 in most states.

Miranda Rule—The law requiring a person receive certain warnings concerning the privilege against self-incrimination, prior to custodial interrogation, as set forth in the landmark case of "*Miranda v. Arizona.*"

Misdemeanor—Criminal offenses that are less serious than felonies and carry lesser penalties.

Mistrial—A trial that is terminated prior to the return of a verdict, such as occurs when the jury is unable to reach a verdict.

Mitigating Circumstances—Circumstances that may reduce the penalty connected with the offense.

Modus Operandi—Latin for "the manner of operation." Refers to the characteristic method used by a criminal in carrying out his or her actions.

Nolo Contendere—Latin for "I do not wish to contend." Statement by a defendant who does not wish to contest a charge. Although tantamount to a plea of guilty for the offense charged, it cannot be used against the defendant in another forum.

Not Guilty—The plea of a defendant in a criminal action denying the offense with which he or she is charged.

Oath—A sworn declaration of the truth under penalty of perjury.

Objection—The process by which it is asserted that a particular question, or piece of evidence, is improper, and it is requested that the court rule upon the objectionable matter.

Obstruction of Justice—An offense by which one hinders the process by which individuals seek justice in the court, such as by intimidating jury members.

Offense—Any misdemeanor or felony violation of the law for which a penalty is prescribed.

Pardon—To release from further punishment, either conditionally or unconditionally.

Parole—The conditional release from imprisonment whereby the convicted individual serves the remainder of his or her sentence outside of prison as long as he or she is in compliance with the terms and conditions of parole.

Penal Institution—A place of confinement for convicted criminals.

Perjury—A crime where a person under oath swears falsely in a matter material to the issue or point in question.

Plea Bargaining—The process of negotiating a disposition of a case to avoid a trial of the matter.

Polygraph—A lie detector test.

Precedent—A previously decided case that is recognized as authority for the disposition of future cases.

Premeditation—The deliberate contemplation of an act prior to committing it.

Presumption of Innocence—In criminal law, refers to the doctrine that an individual is considered innocent of a crime until he or she is proven guilty.

Prisoner—One who is confined to a prison or other penal institution for the purpose of awaiting trial for a crime, or serving a sentence after conviction of a crime.

Probable Cause—The standard which must be met in order for there to be a valid search and seizure or arrest. It includes the showing of facts and circumstances reasonably sufficient and credible to permit the police to obtain a warrant.

Prosecution—The process of pursuing a civil lawsuit or a criminal trial.

Prosecutor—The individual who prepares a criminal case against an individual accused of a crime.

Provocation—The act of inciting another to do a particular deed.

Proximate Cause—That which, in a natural and continuous sequence, unbroken by any efficient intervening cause, produces injury, and without which the result would not have occurred.

Prurient Interest—The shameful and morbid interest in nudity and sex.

Public Defender—A lawyer hired by the government to represent an indigent person accused of a crime.

Racketeering—An organized conspiracy to commit extortion.

Rape—The unlawful sexual intercourse with a female person without her consent.

Reasonable Doubt—The standard of certainty of guilt a juror must have in order to find a defendant guilty of the crime charged.

Restitution—The act of making an aggrieved party whole by compensating him or her for any loss or damage sustained.

Robbery—The felonious act of stealing from a person, by the use of force or the threat of force, so as to put the victim in fear.

Search and Seizure—The search by law enforcement officials of a person or place in order to seize evidence to be used in the investigation and prosecution of a crime.

Search Warrant—A judicial order authorizing and directing law enforcement officials to search a specified location for specific items or individuals.

Self-Defense—The right to protect oneself, one's family, and one's property from an aggressor.

Sentence—The punishment given a convicted criminal by the court.

Separation of Power—The doctrine that prohibits one branch of the government from exercising the powers belonging to another branch of government.

Sequester—Generally, to separate from, such as a jury during trial.

Show Cause Order—An accelerated method of starting an action, brought on by motion, which compels the opponent to respond within a shorter time period than usual.

Status Offender—A child who commits an act which is not criminal in nature, but which nevertheless requires some sort of intervention and disciplinary attention merely because of the age of the offender.

Stay—A judicial order suspending some action until further court order lifting the stay.

Sua Sponte—Latin for "of itself." Refers to an action taken by the court upon its own motion and without the intervention of either party.

Subornation of Perjury—The criminal offense of procuring another to make a false statement under oath.

Suicide—The deliberate termination of one's existence.

Summation—The point in the trial when the attorney for each party sums up the evidence presented in the case, and makes their final argument as to their legal position.

Summons—A mandate requiring the appearance of the defendant in an action under penalty of having judgment entered against him for failure to do so.

Suppression of Evidence—The refusal to produce or permit evidence for use in litigation, such as when there has been an illegal search and seizure of the evidence.

Supreme Court—In most jurisdictions, the Supreme Court is the highest appellate court, including the federal court system.

Suspended Sentence—A sentence that is not executed contingent upon the defendant's observance of certain court-order terms and conditions.

Taking the Fifth—The term given to an individual's right not to incriminate oneself under the Fifth Amendment.

Testify—The offering of a statement in a judicial proceeding, under oath and subject to the penalty of perjury.

Testimony—The sworn statement make by a witness in a judicial proceeding.

Treaty—In international law, refers to an agreement made between two or more independent nations.

Trial—The judicial procedure whereby disputes are determined based on the presentation of issues of law and fact. Issues of fact are decided by the trier of fact, either the judge or jury, and issues of law are decided by the judge.

Trial Court—The court of original jurisdiction over a particular matter.

Unconstitutional—Refers to a statute which conflicts with the United States Constitution rendering it void.

Unfit—Incompetent.

Unreasonable Search and Seizure—A search and seizure that has not met the constitutional requirements under the Fourth and Fourteenth Amendment.

Vacate—To render something void, such as a judgment.

Verdict—The definitive answer given by the jury to the court concerning the matters of fact committed to the jury for their deliberation and determination.

Warrant—An official order directing that a certain act be undertaken, such as an arrest.

White Collar Crime—Refers to a class of non-violent offenses that have their basis in fraud and dishonesty.

Wrongful Death Statute—A statute that creates a cause of action for any wrongful act, neglect, or default that causes death.

Youthful Offender—An individual who is older than a juvenile but younger than an adult.

BIBLIOGRAPHY AND ADDITIONAL RESOURCES

American Civil Liberties Union (ACLU) (Date Visited: March 2008) http://www.aclu.org/.

American Heritage Dictionary of the English Language, Fourth Edition, Boston, MA: Houghton Mifflin Company, 2000.

Amnesty International (AI) (Date Visited: March 2008) http://www.amnesty.org/.

Black's Law Dictionary, Fifth Edition, St. Paul, MN: West Publishing Company, 1979.

Congressional Quarterly Researcher, Volume 5. Washington, DC: Congressional Quarterly, Inc.

Death Penalty Information Center (Date Visited: March 2008) http://www.deathpenaltyinfo.org/.

Federal Bureau of Investigation (Date Visited: March 2008) http://www.fbi.gov/.

Innocence Project (Date Visited: March 2008) http://www.innocenceproject.org/.

National Institute of Mental Health (Date Visited March 2008) http://www.nimh.nih.gov/.

Pro-Death Penalty.com (Date Visited: March 2008) http://www.prodeathpenalty.com/.

U.S. Department of Justice (Date Visited: March 2008) http://www.usdoj.gov/bjs/.

U.S. Department of Justice, Bureau of Justice Statistics (Date Visited: March 2008) http://www.ojp.usdoj.gov/bjs/html/.

U.S. Department of Justice, National Criminal Justice Reference Center (Date Visited: March 2008) http://www.ncjrs.gov/.

U.S. Department of State (Date Visited: March 2008) http://usinfo.state.gov/dhr/human_rights/capital_punishment.html/.